"With this book, Tim Bartik has solidified his rank as the leading, trusted expert on economic development incentives and economic development broadly. The role of firm-based incentives has triggered passionate debate, and Bartik responds with rigor, reason, and realism. I hope readers heed the call for needed reforms recommended in this timely book."
—*Amy Liu, vice president and director, Brookings Metropolitan Policy Program*

"Economic development incentives are one of the biggest boondoggles of our time, draining away tens of billions of dollars of precious taxpayer dollars, with some states and cities offering as much as $7 billion to lure Amazon's much-ballyhooed HQ2. No one understands the intricacies of economic development incentives—what works and what does not—and the broader field of economic development policy and strategy better than Tim Bartik. This book is an absolute must read for mayors, governors, economic developers, city-builders, CEOs and business executives, community activists, and all those concerned about the future of our cities and communities."
—*Richard Florida, author of* The Rise of the Creative Class, *and university professor at the University of Toronto*

"This book needed to be written and Tim Bartik needed to write it. Using clear, simple language and solid, empirical evidence he's collected over decades of close observation, Bartik explains how state and local policymakers can make smart decisions about business incentives, bringing real benefits to their communities and avoiding the next Foxconn."
—*Jared Bernstein served as chief economist to former Vice President Joe Biden, and is a senior fellow at the Center on Budget and Policy Priorities.*

"For just shy of three decades, Tim Bartik has been the country's leading expert on the economics of state and local economic development strategies and programs. In language that is completely accessible to elected officials—not an equation in sight!—he rigorously explains here how to think about the benefits *and* costs of economic development incentives, optimize their structure, and evaluate their effectiveness. Every governor and state legislator should carve out three hours and read this book and then take its teachings to heart."
—*Michael Mazerov, senior fellow, State Policy Project, Center on Budget and Policy Priorities*

Making Sense of Incentives

Making Sense of Incentives
Taming Business Incentives to Promote Prosperity

Timothy J. Bartik

2019

WE *focus* series

W.E. Upjohn Institute for Employment Research
Kalamazoo, Michigan

Library of Congress Cataloging-in-Publication Data

Names: Bartik, Timothy J., author.
Title: Making sense of incentives : taming business incentives to promote prosperity / Timothy J. Bartik.
Description: Kalamazoo, Michigan : W.E. Upjohn Institute for Employment Research, 2019. | Series: WEfocus series | Includes bibliographical references and index. | Summary: "In evaluating incentives, everything depends on the details: how much in incentives it takes to truly cause a firm to locate or expand, the multiplier effects, the effects of jobs on employment rates, how jobs affect tax revenue versus public spending needs. Do benefits of incentives exceed costs? This depends on the details. This book is about those details. What magnitudes of incentive effects are plausible? How do benefits and costs vary with incentive designs? What advice can be given to evaluators? What is an ideal incentive policy? Answering these questions about incentives depends on a model of incentive effects, which this book provides" — Provided by publisher.
Identifiers: LCCN 2019037192 (print) | LCCN 2019037193 (ebook) | ISBN 9780880996686 (paperback) | ISBN 9780880996693 (ebook)
Subjects: LCSH: Industrial promotion—United States. | New jobs tax credit—United States. | Tax incentives—United States. | Industrial policy—United States.
Classification: LCC HC110.I53 B37 2019 (print) | LCC HC110.I53 (ebook) | DCC 338.973—dc23
LC record available at https://lccn.loc.gov/2016037192
LC ebook record available at https://lccn.loc.gov/2019037193

© 2019
W.E. Upjohn Institute for Employment Research
300 S. Westnedge Avenue
Kalamazoo, Michigan 49007-4686

The facts presented in this study and the observations and viewpoints expressed are the sole responsibility of the author. They do not necessarily represent positions of the W.E. Upjohn Institute for Employment Research.

Cover design by Carol A.S. Derks.
Index prepared by Diane Worden.
Printed in the United States of America.
Printed on recycled paper.

Contents

Acknowledgments		xi
Preface		xiii

1 Why Incentives Are Tempting but Problematic — 1
   What We Talk about When We Talk about Incentives — 1
   Why Job Growth? — 2
   Why Targeted Incentives? Political Reasons — 3
   Why Targeted Incentives? Economic Rationale — 4
   Wasteful Incentives — 5
   Evaluating Incentives — 6

2 A Description of Business Incentives — 7
   Incentive Trends — 7
   Incentives Today — 8
   How Large Are Incentives? — 10
   Which Firms Get Incentives? — 12
   Do Incentives Target Needy Areas? — 13
   Long-Term Incentives — 14
   Understanding Incentives — 15

3 Multipliers and Leakages: How to Think about Incentives — 17
   Multipliers and Spillovers — 18
   Leakages and Negative Feedbacks — 22
   Key Factors Affecting Incentive Benefits — 26
   Differences from Usual Incentive Models — 36
   The Devil Is in the Details — 37

4 Improving Incentives: What Can Policymakers Do? — 39
   The Baseline Model — 39
   Why Average Incentives Have Benefits Close to Costs — 45
   Average Incentives Are Dominated by Better Policies — 47
   Better Incentive Policies — 54

5 Are My State's Incentives Working? Practical Evaluation Strategies for Incentive Programs — 61
   Use a Model — 61
   Evaluating Job Creation Effects on Incented Firms: The Selection Bias Challenge — 63

	Overcoming Selection Bias	64
	Surveys	77
	Applying National Studies to State-Specific Incentives	81
	What Should an Evaluator Do?	86
	We Already Know Something about Ideal Policies	88
6	**An Ideal State Incentive Program, Taking Account of Economic and Political Realities**	89
	Principles	89
	An Ideal Program	91
	Possible Questions, with Responses	93
	The State Perspective vs. the National Perspective	98
7	**The National Interest: What Should the Federal Government Do about State and Local Incentives?**	101
	Is State and Local Competition for Jobs a Zero-Sum Game?	102
	Customized Business Services Can Make the National Economic Pie Bigger	104
	Targeting Distressed Areas Can Make the National Economic Pie Bigger and Help the Nonemployed	105
	Targeting High-Tech Clusters Can Make the National Economy More Productive by Augmenting Agglomeration Economies	106
	Rejoining the Real World: Actual Incentive Practice Is Unlikely to Have Net National Benefits	107
	A Simple Solution	108
	Balancing State Sovereignty with National Interests	109
	A National Proposal	111
	Moving on from the Ideal	114
8	**A Practical Path Forward**	115
	Transparency	115
	Evaluation	116
	Alternatives	118
	A Full-Employment Economy	119
	The Baby and the Bathwater	120
Notes		121
References		139
Author		149
Index		151
About the Institute		163

Figures

2.1	Average Incentive Offer as a Percentage of a Firm's Value of Production	8
2.2	Typical State Incentives as a Percentage of a Firm's Value of Production, Various Years after Facility Opening	15
3.1	A Model of Incentives' Benefits	19
3.2	Adding Incentive Costs to the Model	23
4.1	Baseline Income Shares vs. Share of Net Benefits	43
4.2	Benefit-Cost Ratios for Alternative State Policies	50
5.1	"Effects" of Hypothetical Job Growth Program in Michigan Counties, Estimated Using Regression-Discontinuity Design	76

Tables

2.1	Annual State/Local Incentives, by Type of Incentive	9
4.1	Types of Income Benefits for State Residents, as a Ratio to Incentive Costs	42
4.2	Benefit-Cost Ratios of Alternative Incentive Policies	55
6.1	Comparison of Current Incentives vs. "Ideal" Incentives	94

Boxes

5.1	Evaluation of the Washington State High Technology Tax Credit	68
5.2	Questions to See If a Natural Experiment Evaluation Is Feasible	69
5.3	A Regression-Discontinuity Design County Example with Hypothetical Program Effects	75
5.4	Questions to See If a Regression-Discontinuity Design Evaluation Is Feasible	77
5.5	Evaluation of the Massachusetts Workforce Training Fund Program	80
5.6	Factors Enhancing the Credibility of Surveys of Incentive Effects	81
5.7	Two Hypothetical Examples of Using the Tax Research to Estimate Incentive Effects	84
5.8	Evaluation of the Michigan Business Development Program	85
5.9	Summary of Evaluation Options for State Incentive Programs	87
7.1	Summary of Proposed National Economic Development Program	114

Acknowledgments

Support for this project was provided by the Pew Charitable Trusts and the Upjohn Institute. The views expressed herein are those of the author and do not necessarily reflect the views of the the Pew Charitable Trusts or the Upjohn Institute. Research assistance and support for this project was provided by Nathan Sotherland and Claire Black. Helpful comments were provided by Mark Robyn, Jeff Chapman, George Erickcek, Amy Liu, Michael Mazerov, Ken Poole, Richard Florida, Jared Bernstein, and an anonymous reviewer. The manuscript was capably edited by Allison Hewitt Colosky. Other assistance with the publication process was provided by Rich Wyrwa and Brad Hershbein.

Preface

Who is this book for?

In my hopes, this book will interest anyone who wants to encourage economic prosperity for all Americans. Prosperity for all requires sufficient creation of jobs. Job creation is too important to be left to the federal government alone; state and local governments also need to help create jobs.

If you're a governor or mayor, how will you create jobs for your constituents? For most governors and mayors, the main job creation policy is economic development incentives—business tax breaks or other government assistance, which goes to targeted businesses to create jobs in a local area. Any concerned voter should want to understand our current incentive policies—do they make sense as part of our nation's economic policies?

But a primary audience for this book is those who design and use incentives: governors and mayors and their staffs, and state legislators and city council members and their staffs. How can these policymakers better design incentives? How can they avoid excessive incentive costs that threaten other budget priorities?

Another audience is the staff who evaluate incentives: analysts in legislative audit bureaus or executive audit agencies, and researchers within economic development agencies. How should they evaluate incentives? What are the desired benefits of incentives, which an evaluation should seek to objectively measure? What are the possible hidden costs? What evaluation methods are reliable?

Finally, important audiences for this book are those outside the incentive policy world who seek to understand incentives and judge their merits: journalists concerned with state and local government or the local business community; public interest groups and good government groups; and, of course, the public. What information should the public demand from state and local governments? How can they tell whether incentives are succeeding or failing? What should incentives be expected to achieve? How do incentives fit into overall state and local economic development policy?

The policy debate over incentives is full of bad ideas and misleading claims. For example, economic developers sometimes mistakenly claim that incentives tip every location or expansion decision they touch. Economic developers sometimes also mistakenly claim that "incentives pay for themselves"—the gain in state and local tax revenue generated from incentives' job creation is claimed to exceed whatever business tax breaks are handed out.

In this book, I analyze incentives' benefits and costs with an economic model based on empirical evidence. Common claims about incentives are debunked. For example, incentives don't tip every location decision of assisted businesses; research suggests that typical incentives tip less than 25 percent of the location or expansion decisions of assisted businesses. Even without the incentives, the state or local area would have received at least 75 percent of these jobs.

As another example, after one accounts for the public service needs caused by job growth, typical incentives do not pay for themselves. Job growth yields population growth that increases the need for public services, such as expanded roads, more teachers, and police. Such public service needs consume over 90 percent of any increased tax revenue. Incentives only have slight "fiscal benefits" (fiscal benefits are the increase in tax revenue minus the increase in needed public services spending). Such fiscal benefits are not incentives' main benefit.

If an incentive program is to have benefits exceeding costs, the main benefits come from increased earnings per capita of state residents, due to job creation pushing up employment-to-population ratios. But were the incentive costs to achieve this job creation too great? What government spending program was cut or taxes were raised to pay for the incentive costs, and what impact would that alternative use of resources have had on the state economy? Understanding the job creation effects of incentives requires looking beyond the obvious possible effects on the firms receiving incentives. Job creation in a state also is affected by many other state characteristics, including government tax and spending policies.

Economists can be needlessly technical. But the economic concepts can be grasped by any interested reader, if clearly shown. That is my goal in this book. I seek to clarify

- what incentives should be trying to do;
- how best to evaluate incentives' effects; and
- how state, local, and federal policymakers can reform incentives.

With better ideas and evidence, the policy debate over incentives will be more productive. If we want to tame incentives so that they are better targeted at creating jobs for all, we need to first make sense of incentives. Without the right model for understanding incentives, we're unlikely to make much progress in targeting incentives at the right goals. Without knowledge of the empirical facts, state and local policymakers are acting blindly. In this book, I fill these gaps by providing better ideas and models to understand incentives, and by uncovering empirical facts that can guide incentive policy.

Chapter 1
Why Incentives Are Tempting but Problematic

Are economic development incentives out of control?

To attract jobs, state and local governments increasingly provide targeted businesses with incentives: tax breaks, cash grants, free land, free job training. Since 1990, incentives have tripled to $50 billion annually.

Recent incentive offers have escalated:

- In 2017, Wisconsin agreed to provide tech giant Foxconn with incentives of over $3 billion for a new manufacturing plant to make flatscreen panels. The Foxconn deal in Wisconsin was equivalent to paying Foxconn a wage subsidy of 30 percent for 20 straight years.
- In 2017 and 2018, numerous states competed for Amazon's proposed "Headquarters II." Several serious offers exceeded $7 billion.[1]

Having seen what states were willing to offer Foxconn and Amazon, one can easily imagine business incentives mushrooming. Business incentives may increasingly inhibit the ability of state and local governments to provide public services, such as schools and roads.

WHAT WE TALK ABOUT WHEN WE TALK ABOUT INCENTIVES

Economic development incentives are tax breaks, cash grants/loans, or services that are

1) targeted at an individual firm, or some industry or group of firms; and

2) intended to promote job growth in a state, or in a local geographic area that is big enough to be a local labor market.[2]

By "local labor market," I mean an area big enough so that increasing jobs in the area affects job availability for local workers. This size criterion requires that the area be big enough to encompass a substantial share of all local commuting flows. A metropolitan area would clearly be big enough.[3] In contrast, moving jobs from one neighborhood to a bordering neighborhood would not affect job availability for workers because few people work in the same neighborhood they live in. Policies targeting neighborhoods are usually labeled as "community development" policies, not "economic development" policies. Community development policies may provide important benefits by improving neighborhood amenities. But economic development policies aim at affecting job availability for local workers. Job growth only affects job availability for local workers if it affects job growth at a larger geographic scale than the neighborhood.[4]

Anything that state and local governments do—every tax or spending policy, every regulation—might affect job growth. What is distinctive about incentives—and what arouses more controversy—is targeting individual firms or industries, sometimes called "picking winners." Why should a state or local government try to pick winners? Can this targeting strategy achieve a higher "bang for a buck," compared to more general policies to promote job growth? Or is it doomed to make mistakes, or to be corrupted to help political supporters?

WHY JOB GROWTH?

But we're getting ahead of ourselves. First we need to ask: Why promote local job growth? What's wrong with the number of jobs that are produced by the private market on its own, without government intervention?

The private market doesn't produce enough job growth because jobs have social benefits: labor market benefits for state residents, and fiscal benefits that improve state and local governments' budget situations. Private employers ignore these social benefits, and therefore do not expand jobs as much as we would like to see in our society.

Local job growth helps more residents get jobs. This added work experience increases residents' job skills. These greater job skills yield long-run benefits: these local residents will have persistently higher employment rates and earnings.

More jobs also increase state and local tax bases, and thereby increase state and local tax revenue. Governors and mayors have more revenue to work with, without any tax rate hike.

WHY TARGETED INCENTIVES? POLITICAL REASONS

But why pursue local job growth with assistance to targeted firms? Why not just general policies to encourage local job growth?

A *political* reason for incentives is that they are popular. Targeting the creation of particular *identified* jobs—which is what incentives do—is rewarded by voters. Voters are more likely to vote for politicians who offer incentives, even if the incentives are unsuccessful.[5] Voters appreciate well-publicized efforts to attract jobs. If a governor or mayor can go after a prominent large corporation with an incentive offer, why not? At least he is trying; he cares.

Better yet, the incentives may be long-term, paid for by the next governor or mayor. Political benefits now, budget costs later.

A governor or mayor can use the threat of competition from other states and cities to appeal to the minority of voters who are incentive critics. She can say, "Look, I would prefer not to offer large incentives, but I have no real choice except to keep up with the interstate competition."

WHY TARGETED INCENTIVES? ECONOMIC RATIONALE

Incentives also have an *economic* rationale. Targeted assistance to some firms may create more local jobs per dollar than more general policies, for two reasons.

First, targeting some firms may increase their job growth more than spreading the same dollars over all firms. For example, smaller firms often lack information on the latest technology, or on possible new markets. Government services that provide information for small firms may be cheap for the government to provide, yet have large effects on these small firms' growth. Examples of such information services for smaller firms are manufacturing extension services, which offer advice to small- and medium-sized manufacturers on how to improve their competitiveness.

As another example, some firms are actively considering a new location or expansion decision, while other firms have more modest ambitions and are content to stay at the same scale. The former group of firms is easier to affect via government assistance.

Second, targeting job creation on some types of local firms may have higher multiplier effects, which occur when job increases in one local firm lead to job increases in the firm's local suppliers, or in local retailers serving the additional workers. An expansion of an auto final assembly plant leads to increased sales and jobs at local suppliers of auto component parts. The added workers at the assembly plant and the parts suppliers will buy more at local grocery stores and brewpubs, increasing these retailers' jobs.

Multipliers are higher for firms producing "tradable" goods or services. For regional economists, tradable goods or services are more than those sold in international trade—they are any goods and services that are sold outside the *local* economy, such as manufactured goods. For example, Michigan auto plants sell cars to Ohio, so autos would be "tradable" goods for Michigan even if international sales were nonexistent. Nontradable goods or services are sold within the local economy, such as local restaurants. Helping one local restaurant expand will reduce sales and jobs at other local restaurants. This local competition reduces the multiplier, perhaps all the way to zero: any jobs gained at the assisted restaurant may be offset by jobs lost at other local restaurants. In contrast, local manufacturers compete with firms elsewhere, so incentives may help these firms gain a greater share of the national or even international market.

Multipliers are also higher in high-tech industries in local economies that have many other, related high-tech firms.[6] High-tech firms cluster together, as seen in Silicon Valley. Attracting more high-tech firms may help an already-existing local high-tech cluster to grow and prosper.

WASTEFUL INCENTIVES

Incentives can be wasteful. State and local costs may be large, with little local benefit.

First, many incentives have little effect. As we will review, for typical incentives, only a minority of incented firms will be induced to alter their location or expansion decisions. Yes, there is competition from incentives in other states. But even with this competition, typical incentives are small enough as a percent of firms' costs that they rarely drive the location or expansion decision.

Second, multipliers often are smaller than claimed. More local jobs will drive up local wages and prices. Increased wages and prices will drive away some local jobs, reducing the multiplier.

Third, most new local jobs eventually go to in-migrants. Local job growth drives local population growth. This reduces the job opportunities that state residents receive from new jobs.

Fourth, increased jobs and population will increase public spending needs. As we will review, these increased spending needs are almost as large as the tax revenue gain from a larger state and local tax base. Incentives' "fiscal benefits"—the tax revenue gain minus the increased spending needs—are slight, and almost always far less than the dollar costs of incentives. As a result, incentives do not pay for themselves.

Fifth, the net financial costs of incentives, after netting out fiscal benefits, must come from somewhere in state and local budgets. Some taxes must be raised or some public spending cut. Either tax increases or public spending cuts will hurt the local economy. The *economic* costs of incentives are more than their *dollar* costs.

EVALUATING INCENTIVES

Therefore, in evaluating incentives, everything depends on the details: how much in incentives it takes to truly cause a firm to locate or expand, the multiplier effects, the effects of jobs on employment rates, how jobs affect tax revenue versus public spending needs. Do benefits of incentives exceed costs? This depends on the details.

This book is about those details. What magnitudes of incentive effects are plausible? How do benefits and costs vary with incentive designs? What advice can be given to evaluators? What is an ideal incentive policy?

Answering these questions about incentives depends on a model of incentive effects, which this book provides. First, however, the next chapter describes our current incentive practices. How are incentives designed and used by U.S. state and local governments?

Chapter 2
A Description of Business Incentives

INCENTIVE TRENDS

Government incentives for businesses are as American as apple pie or Social Security.[7] Our current state incentive competition began with Mississippi, in 1936. Mississippi's "Balance Agriculture with Industry" program enticed Northern manufacturing facilities to Mississippi by leasing them land and buildings at low rents, without local property taxes.[8] Other Southern states followed, and later Northern and Western states.

The incentive competition escalated in the 1970s and after. Why the escalation? Perhaps the slowdown in growth of U.S. wages. Governors and mayors might have felt pressured to do something to create more and better jobs.

From 1990 to 2015, business incentives tripled (Figure 2.1). Most of this tripling occurred from 1990 to 2001. Since 2001, average business incentives across the nation have been roughly stable. Some high-incentive states, such as New York and Michigan, have made incentive cutbacks. Some low-incentive states, such as Wisconsin, have made incentive expansions. The 2001–2015 stability suggested a temporary political stalemate: proponents and opponents of incentives had roughly offsetting influences.

But where are we headed now? Recent billion-dollar incentive offers to Foxconn and Amazon raise fears that the incentive competition could once again escalate.[9]

8 Bartik

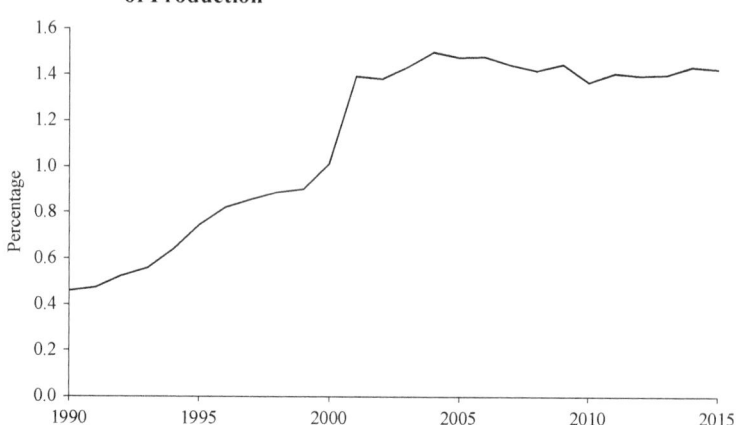

Figure 2.1 Average Incentive Offer as a Percentage of Firm's Value of Production

NOTE: This figure shows average business incentives across U.S. states for firms in tradable industries. The present value of the incentive offer over 20 years is calculated, as a percentage of the present value of the firm's "value of production," or value-added, over those same 20 years. The particularly large jump from 2000 to 2001 comes from New York, but the overall increase from 1990 to 2000 is more broadly based.
SOURCE: Bartik (2017a, p. 69, Figure 3).

INCENTIVES TODAY

Business incentives today have a total cost of around $50 billion annually (Table 2.1).[10]

The largest type of incentives are job creation credits: tax breaks or cash grants that are either some dollar amount per new job or some percentage of the new jobs' wages. Such job creation credits grew from almost nothing in 1990 to almost $20 billion annually today—nearly two-fifths of the total of all incentives. Many job creation credits are so large because states allow firms to simply keep their workers' personal state income tax withholdings. (The worker still gets credited with a payment.) This allows these job creation credits to exceed the firm's state corporate income tax liabilities, which

Table 2.1 Annual State/Local Incentives, by Type of Incentive

Level of government	Type of incentives	Annual dollars (in billions)
Mostly state tax credits/cash payments	Job creation credits	19
	Investment tax credits	7
	R&D tax credits	7
Mostly local tax breaks	Property tax abatements	14
Subtotal for cash incentives (sum of above)		47
Mixed federal/state/local funding	Economic development services	3
	Total	50

NOTE: Figures are in 2018 dollars, updated largely from Bartik (2017a). The cost estimates for business services are derived in Bartik (2019).
SOURCE: Author's calculations.

ordinarily limit how much in tax breaks a firm can take. But state governments can still claim that firms are not being paid state money directly, just keeping some funds they would otherwise pay the state.

Most business incentives are provided by state governments. An exception is property tax abatements, under which local governments forgive all or part of a firm's normal property tax bill for some period. Property tax abatements have long been a prominent incentive, going back to Mississippi's completely forgiving property taxes on new manufacturing plants. Even today, property tax abatements have an annual cost of $14 billion, over one-quarter of the total incentives.

Other tax incentives include investment tax credits and R&D tax credits. Despite the rhetoric about helping high-tech industries, R&D credits are a relatively modest incentive compared to others.

The bulk of incentives are tax incentives, or other cash incentives, over 90 percent or almost $47 billion of the total $50 billion. Tax breaks or cash grants are easy to hand out to any firm.

But some incentives are customized services targeted at individual firms. Such services total over $3 billion per year.

One such service is customized job training, at almost $1 billion per year. Customized job training programs are typically run by local community colleges and are distinctive in seeking to meet the specific training needs of an individual firm. Customized training programs are frequently tied to a new facility opening or an expansion. The community college works with the firm to design the training program and screen job applicants.

Another such customized business service is manufacturing extension, at almost one-half billion per year. State manufacturing extension centers are funded by the federal government with supplements from state and local governments and business fees. These centers mostly work with small and medium-sized manufacturers. What these manufacturers receive from extension centers is advice, which might be on adopting new technology, or identifying new markets, or any other information that might improve the firm's profitability. Some advice is directly provided by center staff; other advice is brokered by the center using networks of consultants at local universities or elsewhere.

Many other customized services go to small businesses in general. Such services include entrepreneurship training, small business development centers, and business incubators. Potential entrepreneurs are provided with training and advice on whether and how to start a successful business. Existing small businesses may be given training and advice on how to expand. Business incubators may provide cheap space along with advice and opportunities for networking. The federal government funds some of this small business assistance, but state governments also provide funding.

HOW LARGE ARE INCENTIVES?

At $50 billion, current business incentives are both large and small, depending on the basis for comparison.

Compared to state corporate income tax revenues of $48 billion annually, business incentives are large.[11] They are also large compared to overall state and local business taxes paid by assisted businesses.

State and local business taxes go beyond state corporate income taxes to include the larger categories of state sales taxes on business inputs and local property taxes. For the average firm receiving incentives, such incentives offset 30 percent of the overall state and local business taxes the firm would otherwise pay.

But business incentives are modest compared to the size of business activity. The average business incentive offer is equivalent to subsidizing 3 percent of the firm's wages for 20 years.[12] Even relatively modest changes in a state's wages or worker productivity could offset incentives.

The modest size of incentives suggests that it would be surprising to find that average incentives have *overwhelming* effects in determining business location decisions. On the other hand, a 3 percent reduction in wages would be expected to have *some* effect. To see this, look at what it takes for incentives to tip location decisions to a particular state—call it YourStateName.[13] Some firms would have chosen YourStateName anyway. YourStateName offering an incentive has no effect on these firms. Other firms, without the incentive, would have chosen SomeOtherState. These are firms whose location decisions can potentially be tipped by YourStateName offering an incentive. Whether an incentive will cause the firm to switch from SomeOtherState to YourStateName depends on the gap in the firm's profitability between SomeOtherState and YourStateName. The average amount of this gap, and its range across different firms, depends on how much costs and therefore profits vary across states. An incentive offer by YourStateName that is 0.01 percent of wages will rarely if ever be enough to offset such gaps, as variation across states in wages, labor productivity, and other costs will usually cause much larger gaps in profits than 0.01 percent of wages between SomeOtherState and YourStateName. On the other hand, a 30 percent of wages incentive would cause more firms to switch from SomeOtherState to YourStateName. (Of course, that might not be a good idea, as the 30 percent of wages incentive is 3,000 times costlier than the 0.01 percent of wages incentive.) A 3 percent of wages incentive by YourStateName is in between; it will tip a few decisions, but many more firms would have chosen YourStateName anyway, and even more firms will still choose SomeOtherState.

Business incentives are also modest compared to overall state and local budgets. Business incentives are about 3 percent of total state and local annual tax revenue of $1.7 trillion.[14] Current average incentives do not substantially affect overall tax burdens or public services. Maybe in some times and places an incentive offer depresses public services, but this is not true on average.

But incentives might become bolder. The Wisconsin Foxconn offer was equivalent to subsidizing 30 percent of Foxconn's wages for 20 years, over 10 times the current average incentive offer. If business incentives were 30 percent of wages, their effects on business location decisions would be much larger.[15] If business incentives cost $500 billion annually—30 percent of total state and local tax revenue—either households would pay a lot more in state and local taxes, or public spending on schools and roads and other local services would suffer.[16]

WHICH FIRMS GET INCENTIVES?

Business incentives mostly go to firms in tradable industries, also known as firms in export-base industries. These are firms that sell their goods and services outside the state. Tradable industries include most manufacturing industries, as well as industries such as software, tourism, mining, farming, etc.

Targeting incentives on tradable-industry firms makes sense. Providing incentives to firms in nontradable industries amounts to subsidizing some local firms to compete with other local firms. Why would a state or local government want to do that?

Among tradable industries, incentives tend to vary, but not in any sensible way that is related to likely incentive benefits. An industry's average incentives are not much correlated with whether the industry pays high wages. An industry's average incentives are not much correlated with whether it is high-tech. For example, among a group of 31 tradable group industries with data on incentives, by far the most high-tech are chemicals manufacturing and computer manufacturing. The R&D spending of these two industries is each over three times that of the average tradable industry. But among the 31 tradable industries, computer manufacturing is ranked 10th in its average level of incentives for the average state, and chemicals manufacturing is ranked 24th.[17] Their high-tech nature wins them no incentive love. This is despite R&D tax credits, which are too small to result in much industry targeting.

Incentives favor large firms. Over 90 percent of incentives go to firms with more than 100 employees; such firms are 66 percent of private jobs.[18] The largest firms benefit most. Wisconsin's Foxconn offer promised annual incentives to this one firm equal to one-third of Wisconsin's total annual incentives to all firms.

Why favor large firms? There are bad reasons and good reasons. Among the bad reasons: governors and mayors know that incentives to large firms get the most media attention. Another bad reason: large firms are more likely to know about incentives, and more likely to have the time and expertise to navigate the application process. But there is at least one good reason for favoring large firms: state economic development agencies may find it administratively efficient. The state government's administrative costs per job incented are lower by targeting large firms: it's cheaper to deal with a few firms, with many jobs at each firm, than to deal with many firms, with few jobs at each firm.

DO INCENTIVES TARGET NEEDY AREAS?

Incentives vary greatly by state. New Mexico's incentives are about three times the national average. The state of Washington's incentives are less than 10 percent of the national average.[19]

But state variation in incentive offers does not seem to have much to do with which states might need jobs more. Indiana's incentives are twice as high as Illinois's; the two states are similar in their employment-to-population ratio. South Carolina's incentives are twice as high as North Carolina's, for no obvious economic reason.[20] This lack of targeting seems to cry out for reforms, which I advocate in this book.

The best predictor of a state's incentives is what it did last year. State incentives persist until some governor or legislator makes an abrupt change, which may have more to do with politics than economics. Political gamesmanship leads to states making incentive changes, not changes in the state's need for more jobs. Each new governor needs to mark his territory by tweaking his state's incentives.

Within states, most incentives are generally available. There is little effective targeting of local labor markets that lack jobs.[21] State governments, which dominate incentive policy, find it hard to pick geographic winners and losers. Each state legislator wants state incentives to benefit her district.

LONG-TERM INCENTIVES

Policymakers have choices about how incentives are structured over time for a new or expanding firm. They can pay incentives only in the first years of an investment, or over a much longer period.

Incentives are front-loaded, to some degree (Figure 2.2). They are highest in the first year of a new or expanded plant but persist at a high level through the new plant's year 10.

Long-term incentives are a problem, for two reasons. First, long-term incentives may be less effective per dollar. Firms are focused on short-term profits. The incentive in year 10 probably doesn't affect location decisions. Why, then, do governors and mayors offer such long-term incentives?

Second, long-term incentives are more likely to be paid by the next governor or mayor. This helps explain why governors and may-

A Description of Business Incentives 15

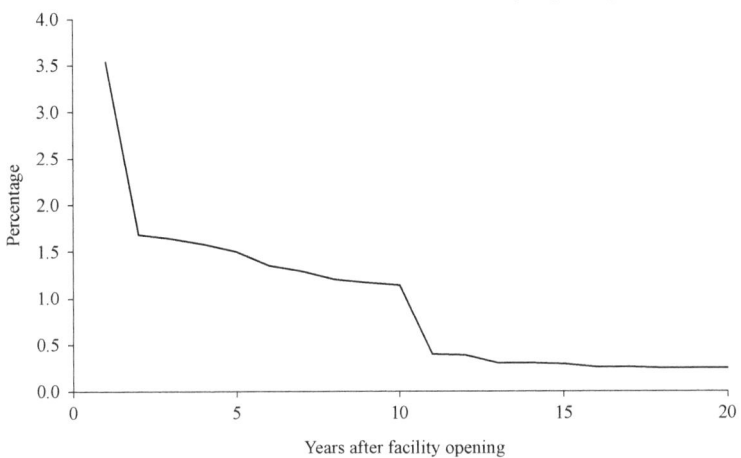

Figure 2.2 Typical State Incentives as a Percentage of a Firm's Value of Production, Various Years after Facility Opening

NOTE: This figure shows average state/local incentives for a new facility, in years 1 through 20 of the new facility's operation, as a percentage of the facility's value-added in each year.
SOURCE: Bartik (2017a, p. 82).

ors offer long-term incentives. But this means that incentive decisions are being made with inadequate concern for long-term costs. Long-term incentives offer political benefits now, and future leaders will have to figure out how to pay for them. Is it any wonder that this political calculation tempts governors and mayors to offer long-term incentives that are excessively costly?

UNDERSTANDING INCENTIVES

Better targeting and design of incentives requires better evaluation of incentives' benefits and costs. Evaluation must be based on analyzing incentives with a good model. I now turn to a conceptual model for how incentives affect a state's residents.

Chapter 3
Multipliers and Leakages
How to Think about Incentives

How should we evaluate incentives' benefits and costs?[22] That depends on incentives' goals.

Let's start with a state perspective. Chapter 7 will consider a national perspective. But states are the main actors in the current incentive wars. From an individual state's perspective, what should governors and state legislators be trying to do with incentives? Presumably, helping state residents. Incentive costs and incentive-induced jobs affect state residents in many ways. Job growth may sometimes harm the environment. More and different people in a state may affect the quality of life, in ways both good and bad.

But incentives' most important effects are on state residents' per capita incomes—both average per capita incomes and the distribution of income across different income groups. I don't mean to sound like an economist obsessed with money, but higher per capita incomes are important to peoples' well-being.

Furthermore, we know a lot about how job growth affects income; how growth affects the local quality of life is harder to measure. Quality of life effects also may vary quite a bit with the state's circumstances and the particular job creation project. Generalizing about quality of life effects may not be feasible.

Therefore, I focus on how the level and distribution of state residents' per capita incomes are affected. The reader should keep in mind that job growth may also affect a state's quality of life in other ways. Ideally, we would adjust our estimates of income effects for these harder-to-measure effects, whether positive or negative.

So, what is the logic for how incentives affect state residents' per capita incomes?

MULTIPLIERS AND SPILLOVERS

Let's start with the positive. Why might incentives increase state residents' incomes? (Negative costs for state residents' incomes will be considered later in this chapter.)

To see the effects of incentives, envision the state economy as a machine. Incentives are a fuel that can set the machine going. The machine of the state economy has various mechanisms that transmit the incentives' fuel into the machine's output: various goodies for the state's residents. Some of these transmission mechanisms may even multiply the effects of the incentive fuel on the machine's ability to produce goodies. Later on, we consider leakages in the machine, which slow down the machine and reduce its production of goodies.

Incentives have several multipliers and spillovers that increase state per capita income (Figure 3.1).[23] Some incentives will directly benefit state residents who own businesses receiving incentives, but most incentives go to out-of-state corporations.[24] How can helping out-of-state corporations ever benefit a state's residents?

For most incentives, benefiting state residents requires that the incentive induce some local job creation. This job creation could be induced in several ways: because of the incentive, a business chooses to locate in the state rather than some other state. Or because of the incentive, a new business is created that would not have occurred otherwise. Or because of the incentive, a business chooses to expand in the state, and otherwise that expansion would not have taken place. Or because of the incentive, a business retains its current jobs in the state, rather than downsizing or closing. In each case, the incentive leads to some additional jobs in the state that would not have existed in the state "but for" the incentive.

An economic developer might say: "What I do must have some impact. Surely you have to admit that providing tax breaks must have *some* impact on the probability of favorable location and expansion decisions made by business executives. The "but for" percentage for incentives must be greater than zero." The "but for" percentage also

Figure 3.1 A Model of Incentives' Benefits

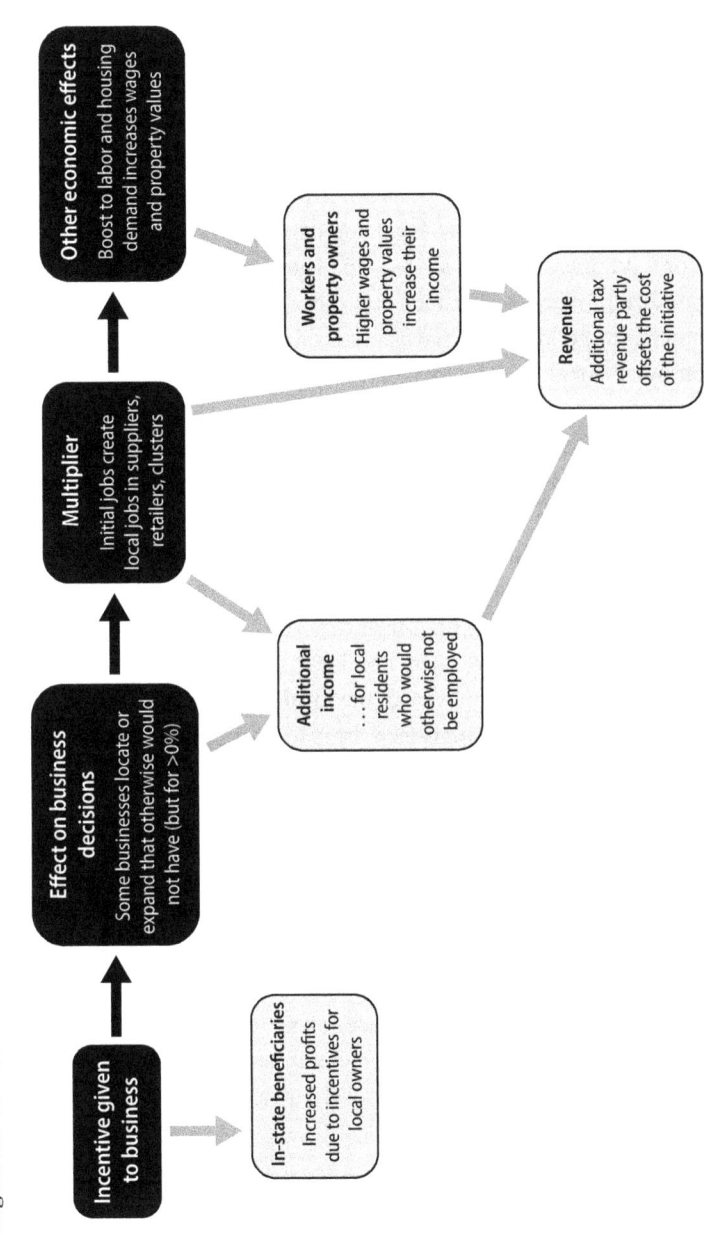

```
Incentive given to business
  │
  ├──> In-state beneficiaries
  │    Increased profits due to incentives for local owners
  │
  ▼
Effect on business decisions
Some businesses locate or expand that otherwise would not have (but for >0%)
  │
  ├──> Additional income
  │    ...for local residents who would otherwise not be employed
  │
  ▼
Multiplier
Initial jobs create local jobs in suppliers, retailers, clusters
  │
  ├──> Revenue
  │    Additional tax revenue partly offsets the cost of the initiative
  │
  ▼
Other economic effects
Boost to labor and housing demand increases wages and property values
  │
  ▼
Workers and property owners
Higher wages and property values increase their income
  │
  ▼
Revenue
Additional tax revenue partly offsets the cost of the initiative
```

may not be 100 percent, but it is realistic to acknowledge the economic developer's point that it is greater than zero.

Job creation in the incented firm will have some multiplier effects. The incented firm may buy more from local suppliers, which will in turn hire more. Workers at the incented firm, and its local suppliers, will have more earnings to spend. Some of these workers' increased earnings may be spent at local companies: grocery stores, hardware stores, restaurants, gift shops, etc. These local companies may hire more employees to distribute their goods and services. If any of these purchased goods and services are produced locally (craft beer? local farmers? local jewelry makers?), then such local production jobs increase.

If the incented firm is high-tech, and there are many other nearby high-tech firms, there may be additional multiplier effects. High-tech firms often cluster. Why this clustering? High-tech firms such as Google steal ideas from one another. Google does so in part by stealing workers from other high-tech firms.[25] If an incentive induces local job creation in a high-tech firm, this additional high-tech firm can contribute more workers and ideas to the local high-tech cluster. This adds to the productivity of the local high-tech cluster, which will encourage other local high-tech firms to start up or expand.[26]

The total boost to local jobs, from both incented firms and their multiplier jobs, will make it easier for state residents to find jobs. The local employment-to-population ratio—the "employment rate"—will go up in the short run. Local workers who otherwise would not have a job end up with additional job experience. A worker who gains job experience will gain job skills. Those added job skills are of many types: from my job experience, I learn how to work with industrial machinery, I gain self-confidence, I am less likely to get involved with alcohol and drugs, and so on. All these added job skills make me more employable in the long run. My long-run employment rate and wage rate will be higher.

This job growth will also boost wages for workers in general, with more labor demand relative to labor supply. This boost in wages would exceed any increases in local consumer prices; an economist would say that local "real wages," wages adjusted for local prices, will increase. Because of both higher employment rates and wages, state residents will experience an increase in per capita earnings.

This increase in per capita earnings is likely to be a higher percentage boost in income for state residents who otherwise would have low and moderate incomes. Low- and moderate-income Americans are more likely to be unemployed, or so discouraged by poor job prospects that they give up seeking jobs. They are also more likely to be underemployed, working in lower-wage jobs than they are capable of doing. Job creation, by increasing employment rates and wages, particularly helps these nonemployed or underemployed Americans. An economist would say that the distribution of earnings gains from local job growth is likely to be "progressive," which is simply jargon for the income boost being a higher percentage of income for those lower in the income distribution.

Growth will increase housing demand. Higher housing demand will boost property values. State residents who own real estate will experience a capital gain.

These capital gains from higher property values are likely to be a higher percentage of income for state residents who are higher in the income distribution, as higher-income Americans are more likely to be homeowners. An economist would say that the distribution of local real estate capital gains from job growth is "regressive," which is simply another way of saying that the boost to economic well-being is a greater percentage of income for those higher in the income distribution. This regressivity is moderate, as home ownership does extend, at lower rates, into lower-income groups.

(What dominates, the progressivity of earnings gains, or the regressivity of property value gains? Stay tuned until the next chapter!)

The increase in business activity and profits, sales, worker earnings, and property values all will increase various tax bases. Revenue for state and local governments will increase, even with no change in tax rates. If nothing else changes, this provides a fiscal benefit for state and local governments.

This fiscal benefit in turn helps state residents. State and local governments have more or less binding balanced budget requirements—they will use this fiscal benefit to either lower residents' tax rates or increase spending on public services or welfare programs that transfer income to state residents. Either way, one could argue that state residents' true incomes per capita, adjusted for government policy, will increase. Lower tax rates obviously increase state residents' net incomes after subtracting taxes. Higher welfare benefits also increase state residents' incomes. Higher public services increase state residents' well-being—which we could view as their "real income"—in that they provide state residents with some service they value: the roads have fewer potholes, the state parks have better and more accessible trails, more policemen and firemen make life a little safer.

In sum, state residents' incomes increase because of higher employment rates, higher wage rates, higher property values, and either lower tax rates or higher public services.

LEAKAGES AND NEGATIVE FEEDBACKS

But the machine of the state economy has various leakages. Incentives' boost to state per capita incomes is reduced or eliminated by several leakages or negative feedbacks (Figure 3.2).

The "but for" percentage is less than 100 percent. Not all firms receiving incentives were induced to locate, expand, or retain jobs because of the incentive. Even without any incentives, many of these firms would have chosen this state anyway. Many other state and local characteristics and national forces affect business decisions—local wage rates, skills of local workers, the area's access to national markets, and so on. A typical incentive, which is equivalent to a 3 percent wage subsidy, will not overwhelm these other forces.

Figure 3.2 Adding Incentive Costs to the Model

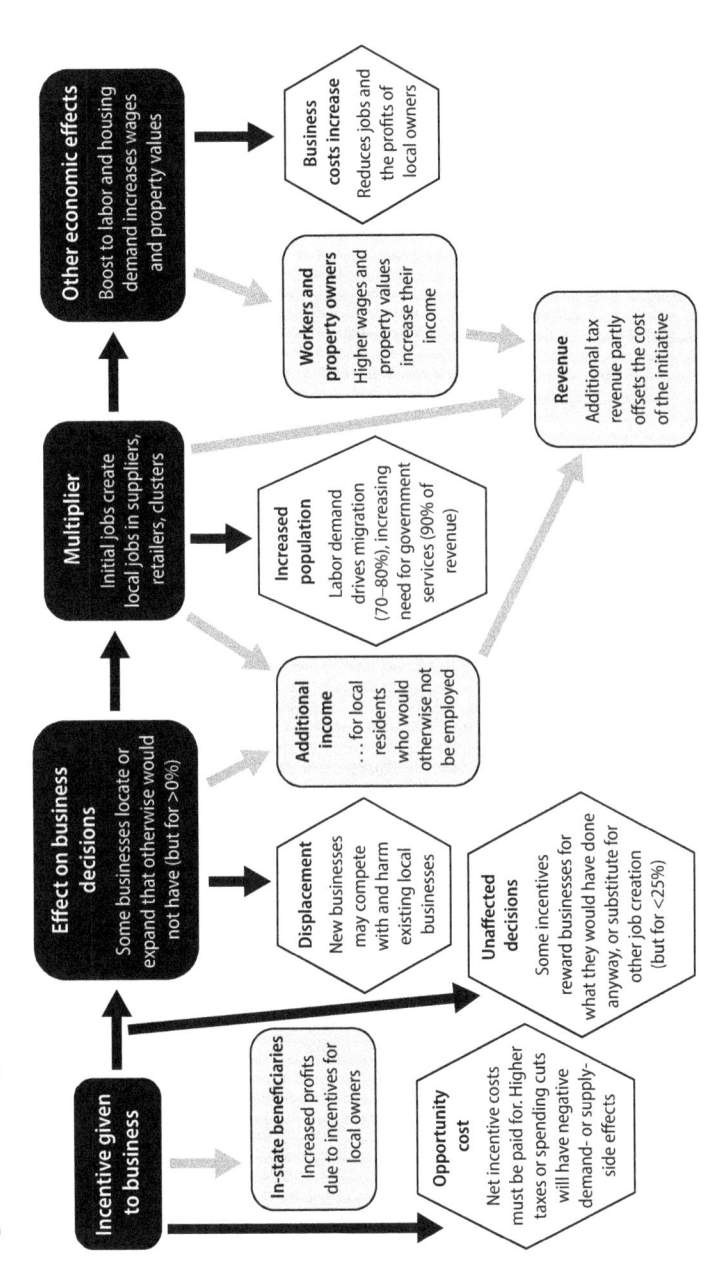

As mentioned previously, incentives to nontradable firms will displace jobs at other local nontradable firms. For firms that sell to a local market, their expansion takes away sales and jobs from other firms selling to the local market. The new local hardware store cuts into the sales of nearby hardware stores.

One might think that wise policymakers would never provide cash incentives to nontradable firms. But incentives are often provided to business activities that are in part nontradable. Witness government subsidies for sports teams. If we're trying to increase total local jobs, such subsidies make little sense.[27] Any expanded jobs at the sports stadium in large part come from local residents spending more at the stadium. This leaves less local disposable income for other local goods and services. Jobs at the stadium and at nearby bars and restaurants may go up, but jobs in other neighborhoods' restaurants and bars, and other local retailers, will go down.

Even for tradable firms, multiplier effects may be less than expected. Increased local wages and property prices will increase business costs. These increased business costs will cause other businesses not to locate or expand in the area. For example, high costs in Silicon Valley and other high-tech areas may drive away many non-tech businesses. In addition, these increased business costs may make local suppliers less competitive and result in increased use of suppliers outside the local area.

Increased business costs reduce profits for some businesses owned by local residents. Businesses that sell locally may be able to pass on increased costs to local consumers.[28] But businesses that sell nationally have their prices set nationally, so they must absorb the business cost increases. A manufacturer in Grand Rapids, Michigan, selling to customers in Chicago or Germany will simply have to absorb any higher costs if Grand Rapids happens to experience a growth boom. These losses to local business owners tend to be much higher for upper-income residents, who are far more likely to own a business.

Not all the jobs that are created in the state will go to residents. Job growth increases population growth. In-migrants will take some of the new jobs.

This in-migration also reduces upward wage pressures. Labor supply increases will to some extent offset the increase in labor demand.

Increased population also raises the demand for government-provided goods and services. In-migrants want good schools for their children. New schools will have to be built and additional teachers hired to avoid increases in class size. New population creates congestion on roads and other local public infrastructure. If we want to avoid increased congestion, we have to spend more on infrastructure. All of this reduces fiscal benefits from incentives.

If state and local governments refuse to increase spending, then state residents are hurt in another way—by reduced quality of public services through more crowded schools and roads. Increased population has costs regardless of state and local policy: policymakers can just choose what form those costs take, either increased needs for spending or reduced local public service quality. Pick your poison.

If the combination of incentive costs plus increased tax revenue, minus increased spending needs, is on net a negative cost for state and local governments, then policymakers will have to keep the budget balanced and pay for these costs. Taxes must go higher, or public spending lower. Either option may have negative effects on the state economy. On the demand side of the economy, higher taxes or lower public spending will reduce state residents' disposable incomes. Lower disposable incomes of state residents will reduce demand for goods and services, which will hurt some businesses in the state and hence hurt their workers.

Higher taxes or lower public spending may also affect the state economy on the supply side. Higher business tax rates may cause other firms to avoid locating or expanding in the state. Cuts in some types of public spending may reduce the productivity of the state economy, and thus reduce state residents' wages and earnings. Cuts in education and job training may reduce skills of state residents, which will reduce their future wages.

KEY FACTORS AFFECTING INCENTIVE BENEFITS

What is the likely magnitude of these multipliers and leakages, these spillovers and negative feedbacks? How are these magnitudes affected by policy?

"But For" Percentage

Research suggests the "but for" percentage is usually less than 25 percent.[29] What does this mean? For a new facility location or expansion decision, this means that the incentive tipped the location decision toward this state only 25 percent of the time or less. The other 75 percent of the time, the firm would have made the same new facility location decision, or same expansion decision, even if no incentive had been provided. Another way to put it: even if the state had not provided incentives to a firm providing a "Big Number" of jobs, 75 percent of those jobs would have been created in the state anyway.[30]

This low "but for" percentage greatly increases the costs of incentives relative to their benefits. At least 75 percent of the time, incentives are all costs, with no job creation benefits.[31] And these incentive costs will require increased state and local taxes, or higher state and local public spending, either of which will have negative economic effects.

Incentive effectiveness can be increased by making incentives more up front.[32] Business executives making investment decisions have an exaggerated focus on the short run, on what happens to profits in the next few years.[33] The incentive provided 10 years from now has little effect on tipping the location or expansion decision. By then, the executive making the location or expansion decision may be long gone. Compared to our typical incentive structure, which continues incentives at a high level through at least 10 years, up-front incentives would be over one-third more effective: per dollar of incentive, the "but for" percentage would be over one-third higher.[34]

Customized services to smaller businesses tend to be far cheaper per assisted job. It would be difficult or impossible to provide useful services to smaller businesses as big as Foxconn-level wage subsidies of 30 percent, or even as big as average business tax incentives. Yet even at much lower costs, customized services to smaller businesses can have considerable effects. Advice to small business is cheap, and—if high-quality—can be effective if used as directed. For these customized services, research shows that the ratio of job creation effects to costs is plausibly 10 times as great as for cash incentives.[35]

In other words, if we reallocated a given dollar amount of our incentive budget away from up-front tax incentives to large corporations, and toward provided customized job training or manufacturing extension services to smaller businesses, we would induce the creation of at least 10 times as many jobs. However, at some point we might face limitations on how much can usefully be spent on customized services to smaller businesses. It might not be as great as the total $50 billion incentive budget, although it is plausibly much greater than the current $3 billion devoted to such services. Advice is useful, but spending 17 times as much on advice is not necessarily 17 times more useful.

Multipliers

Many impact studies done for state economic development agencies estimate multiplier effects of 2.5–4.0. For every job created in incented firms, 1.5–3.0 other jobs are created in other state firms; the multiplier, or ratio of total jobs created to jobs created in incented firms, would then be 2.5–4.0.

Recent research shows that these multipliers are overstated.[36] These studies' multipliers typically focus only on the positive impacts from increased demand for local suppliers and retailers. These studies overlook negative feedback effects from higher costs: higher costs in the state will reduce the state's competitiveness in attracting business growth.[37] Negative feedback effects reduce demand-oriented multipliers by at least one-third.

Plausible state multipliers for most incented firms are around 1.7–2.0.[38] For every 10 jobs directly created by incentives, 7–10 additional jobs will be indirectly created in the state, after allowing for both demand effects, and negative effects of higher costs.

Multipliers may be higher for high-tech firms in high-tech-oriented local economies because of cluster effects. Recent research suggests that such extra cluster effects are concentrated in the relatively few local economies where high-tech clusters are significantly above average size.[39] The existing high-tech cluster need not be as large as Silicon Valley's—a high-tech concentration like Denver or the Twin Cities is enough to cause higher multipliers. On the other hand, out of the approximately 700 local labor markets in the United States, only 60 or so probably have sufficiently large concentrations of high tech to expect significantly higher high-tech multipliers. These are the local labor markets in which the share of employment in high-tech industries is at least one-third greater than in the average community. Most of these high-tech cluster communities are above average in population.[40]

In such high-tech cities, the job multiplier for a new high-tech firm may be as large as 3.0.[41] In contrast, in cities with an average or below high-tech sector, high-tech multipliers are no larger than for other firms. States may make incentives more efficient by targeting high tech, but only for the relatively few high-tech cities—targeting high tech does not work if one is building an area's high-tech sector from scratch, or even if one's high-tech sector is at the U.S. average. Not everywhere can be Silicon Valley or a biotech center.

Multipliers are higher on average if the incentives go to locally owned firms. Locally owned firms, compared to otherwise similar non–locally owned firms, are more likely to use local suppliers.[42] A locally owned bookstore is more likely than a Barnes and Noble bookstore to use a local accountant. In addition, the incentives will increase the profits of local owners, who will spend some of these profits locally, further increasing local jobs. The net effect: for two otherwise similar projects, the project with incentives going to local owners might have a multiplier higher by 5–10 percent, or would be 2.0 rather than 1.85.

Multipliers are also higher if the local economy has high rates of unemployment or nonemployment. With more available local labor, employers are better able to hire locally, which increases the number of new jobs created. An economically depressed area, compared to a booming area,[43] might have a multiplier higher by around 15 percent—in other words, rather than being 1.75, it might be 2.0.

Who Gets the Jobs?

In the short run, in the average state's economy, for every 10 new jobs created, 6 jobs increase the employment-to-population ratio and 4 jobs go to in-migrants. But after five or six years, the proportion increasing the employment-to-population ratio declines to 10–30 percent—for every 10 new jobs, 1–3 jobs increase the employment rate for state residents, and the other 7–9 jobs go to in-migrants. This change over time is due to increased in-migration effects over time. But these effects after 5–6 years seem quite persistent, through at least 15–20 years.[44]

On the one hand, it is surprising to many economists that these labor market effects of more jobs are so persistent. A once-and-for-all increase in a state's jobs has long-term effects in increasing state residents' employability, which will boost long-run earnings. Good economic fortune in the short run alters economic fates in the long run. If you add up the increased earnings from a higher employment-to-population ratio over many years, you end up with a sizable increase in lifetime earnings.

On the other hand, only a minority of new jobs benefit a state's residents. Most new jobs go to in-migrants. These in-migrants are fine people, but they were not the people who paid to finance the state's incentive program. In addition, it is likely that the gain to in-migrants is minor—if these new jobs had not been created in this state or local economy, the in-migrants could have found jobs somewhere else.[45]

It might seem surprising that so few jobs go to the original residents and so many to in-migrants. What if a new incented firm hires all local residents? What needs to be understood is that ultimately, new jobs in a state economy must go to either state residents who would otherwise not be employed, or to new residents—there is no other choice. Mathematically, if one increases state employment, either the employment-to-population ratio goes up, or the population goes up—or, more likely, some combination of the two.

In the real world, the way this plays out is that if a firm hires state residents who are already employed, this creates a job vacancy chain. The new hires create job vacancies at the firms where the residents were previously employed. In turn, these firms make job hires from some combination of three groups: 1) state residents who are *already employed*, 2) state residents who are not employed, 3) in-migrants. Any subsequent hire of state residents who are already employed creates another vacancy, which is filled in the same three ways. The resulting vacancy chain is terminated only by the hiring of either a nonemployed state resident or an in-migrant. Because of these vacancy chains, the ultimate impact on state residents' employment rates, versus in-migration, depends on many factors in addition to whom the incented firm hires.[46] We need to consider the hiring practices of all the firms that are part of the job vacancy chain.

How can policy increase the proportion of new jobs going to state residents?[47] One way is by targeting incentives at places with an excess supply of labor: economically depressed areas.[48] When a local economy's unemployment rate is high, or its labor force participation rates are low, a higher proportion of new jobs go to local residents and a lower proportion to in-migrants. In local economies that are persistently depressed, compared to local economies that are doing well, the proportion of new jobs going to local residents goes up about two-thirds. If the proportion of new jobs going to local residents was 15 percent in the economically booming local economy, it would be 25 percent, two-thirds higher, in the economically depressed local economy. Why are the local employment rate effects higher? Because with more available local residents who are nonemployed, many of whom will have competitive job skills, firms all along the job vacancy chain become more likely to hire a local, nonemployed resident rather than a local resident who is employed or someone from out of state.

Because of both higher local hiring and higher multipliers in distressed areas, targeting distressed areas not only has more progressive benefits, by helping the nonemployed more, but also has greater economic benefits for a state's economy. (Chapter 4 will have some bottom line numbers.) A state targeting needy areas is like the joke about the early Quakers in Philadelphia: they came to do good but ended up doing very well indeed.

Effects on state residents' employment rates can also be increased by policies that encourage incented firms and other firms to hire more state residents who lack jobs. State and local governments can use carrots or sticks to do this. One possible carrot is providing high-quality customized job training services. The local community college can provide training programs customized to firms' skill needs. Those programs can include local residents who lack jobs. Business participation in such programs is likely to increase the proportion of new hires who are local residents who lack jobs. The ultimate impact will be to reduce the hiring of in-migrants, and to make local residents more competitive in the labor market because of their greater job experience.

Another carrot is offering some incentives that are specifically tied to hiring the nonemployed. A problem is that some employers may be reluctant to hire the unemployed. These employers may stigmatize the unemployed as being less-productive workers. For example, one experiment showed that if welfare recipients informed prospective employers that the employer would receive a subsidy for hiring them—which thereby informed the employer that they were on welfare—then this hiring subsidy actually reduced the chances of the welfare recipient being hired.[49]

Therefore, incentives to hire the nonemployed are likely to be more effective if integrated into job training programs that help screen and train the nonemployed, which will help reduce stigma effects. Only the unemployed who go through this screening and training would be eligible for a hiring subsidy, thereby reducing employer fears about the unemployed being unproductive. These job training programs also can screen employers. Employers who do not stigmatize the unemployed can be recruited and therefore are more likely to respond positively to a subsidy for such hiring. Only such recruited employers would be offered a hiring subsidy. In the 1980s, Minnesota ran such a program on a large scale, with some evidence of success.[50]

A stick is accompanying all incentives with a local hiring requirement. Because of fears of driving away businesses, state and local policymakers tend to use a light tap with these sticks. Some local areas, such as Berkeley, have "first source" requirements for firms receiving incentives: such firms are required, for *entry-level* job openings, to *consider* as a first source referrals from local job training agencies. Local hiring is not required for all job openings; it is only encouraged for some job openings.

What Is a Local Economy?

As discussed above, when a local economy is depressed, multiplier effects are larger, and a higher proportion of the new jobs go to local residents. But what is the size of a meaningful local economy? A metropolitan area? A neighborhood?

The best answer is somewhere between a neighborhood and a metropolitan area. A typical U.S. county might be around the right size, in terms of land area, to make a meaningful local labor market. Research suggests that a significant proportion of the increased earnings per capita from increases in job growth within a county will occur within that county.[51] Some labor market benefits will spill over into surrounding counties in the metropolitan area, but enough benefits will remain in the county for the county's labor market conditions to be meaningfully affected. In contrast, for a city neighborhood, most of the benefits of new jobs spill over into surrounding neighborhoods. Targeting jobs at a high-unemployment neighborhood does not target jobs at the neighborhood's residents. Such targeting might mainly increase neighborhood rents, encouraging the neighborhood to gentrify and turn over to higher-income residents.

What if policymakers want to target within a county? They might want to target more new jobs for disadvantaged individuals in disadvantaged neighborhoods. Such targeting is better accomplished through local job training programs or hiring incentives. Just plopping down jobs in a neighborhood is ineffective.[52]

Fiscal Benefits

Incentives may provide state and local governments with some fiscal benefits: gains in tax revenue, due to an expanded tax base, that exceed the increase in public service needs, due to an expanded population. However, these fiscal benefits are usually small enough that incentives are unlikely to pay for themselves: the fiscal benefits will be less than the incentive costs.

Fiscal benefits from incentives will vary greatly, based on local circumstances. If local roads and schools are already congested, then growth will require expensive new infrastructure. If existing infrastructure has plenty of capacity, these infrastructure costs will be less.

But on average, increased public spending needs are likely to use up at least 90 percent of increased state and local tax revenue. As we have discussed, a state's population growth in the long run will likely be 70–90 percent as great as a state's job growth. State and local spending needs in the long run, other things equal, will tend to track population growth. (Whether there is excess capacity in current infrastructure may push spending needs up or down relative to population growth.) Total income in the state will grow along with job growth. State and local tax revenue grows somewhat slower than overall state income: state income tax rates don't go up much with income; consumption of goods covered by the sales tax lags income growth; property tax revenue increases are often restricted by state property tax limitations. Therefore, state and local tax revenue is likely to grow somewhat slower than job growth. The net effect is that public spending needs will tend to be at least 90 percent of revenue growth and may exceed revenue growth if expensive new infrastructure is needed.

The upshot of all this is that incentives are not a free lunch—they must be paid for. Incentives must be financed in some way, by raising state and local taxes, or by cutting state and local public spending.

Opportunity Costs

As already mentioned, the higher taxes or lower public spending used to pay for the net costs of incentives will affect a state's economy in two ways: demand-side effects and supply-side effects. The demand-side effects are the effects of higher taxes or higher spending on demand by consumers for local goods and services. The supply-side effects are the effects of higher business taxes or productive public services on the supply of capital or labor to the state economy. Of all these opportunity costs of paying for incentives, the most important, because they are the largest and most persistent, are the opportunity costs of reducing spending on productive public services.

Demand-side financing effects of incentives are moderate. For example, in the baseline model that will be presented in the next chapter, paying for the net cost of incentives, after allowing for fiscal benefits, via household tax increases offsets about 7 percent of the net job creation induced by incentives.[53] The intuition is that demand-side effects are only temporary. While the incentive is being paid for, the added taxes reduce demand for goods and services. But this effect is temporary; it goes away after the higher taxes used to pay for the incentive are over, whether that takes 5 years or 10 years. And it takes at least tens of thousands in added taxes to reduce demand sufficiently to destroy one job.[54] In contrast, the induced jobs from incentives, and their multiplier effects, are more permanent. A similar argument can be made for the demand-side effects of reduced consumer spending due to lower public spending: the demand-side effects on the state's economy are temporary; these temporary effects do not count for as much as the more persistent effects from incentives.

Supply-side effects from higher business taxes are more persistent but are modest in size relative to the potential effects of business incentives. Most firms paying higher business taxes are producing nontradable goods and services. Firms in nontradable industries base their business activity not on local business taxes but on local demand. The number of jobs in fast-food restaurants depends on the local population size and its income, not on how much in taxes McDonalds pays.

In addition, many firms are not currently considering any investment decisions. The average business is satisfied with its status quo scale of operations. For those firms, moderately higher business taxes will not have the potential for tipping many investment decisions. In contrast, incentives target tradable-industry firms that are currently making location or expansion decisions. As a result, a given dollar amount of incentives has higher job creation effects than a given dollar amount of reductions in general business taxes.

Furthermore, incentives target firms in tradable industries, which have much higher multiplier effects than firms in nontradable industries. An auto company locating or expanding a plant will create many jobs in suppliers and local retailers. Incentivizing a local McDonalds to expand or start up a new facility will destroy as many jobs as it creates by reducing sales at the nearby Burger King.

But as we will see, the opportunity costs of incentives are large if the incentives are financed by cutting productive public spending. Axing needed roads or education has large and extremely persistent effects in damaging the state economy. This will be explored in more detail in Chapter 4.

DIFFERENCES FROM USUAL INCENTIVE MODELS

This model of incentives' benefits and costs differs greatly from commonly used state models. Most states only look at the revenue benefits of incentives for state governments. This is incomplete even for an analysis restricted to fiscal benefits. It overlooks revenue effects on local governments. More importantly, commonly used state models overlook effects on spending needs for state and local public services.

For example, the Legislative Fiscal Bureau for the state of Wisconsin, in evaluating the Foxconn deal, made headlines with its conclusion that the deal wouldn't fiscally break even for the state until 2042.[55] This news was a big political negative for the Foxconn deal.

But even this negative fiscal analysis was overly optimistic. The Fiscal Bureau ignored that the additional jobs and people from the Foxconn deal will require additional public services and hence public spending. Yet even if we ignore local schools, counties, and other local governments, this makes no sense. The state of Wisconsin has revenue-sharing programs for local governments. The state pays a substantial share of the K–12 school bill. It shares in infrastructure costs. A sensible fiscal benefits analysis cannot act as if growth is all revenue gain and no expenditure costs.

Even more importantly, common state models of incentives overlook economic benefits. States are not businesses seeking to make a profit. States do not exist to make money; they exist to serve the interests of state residents. These residents are interested in more and better job opportunities. It is bizarre to analyze any program aimed at increasing job growth, which is pursued to improve residents' job opportunities, and then to ignore such effects in the benefit-cost analysis.

Commonly used models also explicitly or implicitly assume that the "but for" for any incented firm is 100 percent—none of the incented jobs, or any substitutes for those jobs, would have occurred in the state without the incentives. If one assumes incentives are 100 percent successful, is it any wonder that many evaluations of incentives are positive?[56]

Economic developers sometimes argue that tax incentives have zero costs for the government and state residents. As one economic developer said, "It is important to understand that incentives . . . are not 'giving away' tax dollars, they are just taking away fewer of the company's dollars by reducing some of their taxes for a period of time."[57] So, rather than losing tax dollars, we are actually gaining tax dollars from the taxes we still collect on this new firm: "For every dollar we 'did not take' from this company in taxes to incentivize them to come to our community we will collect $22 in new taxes—new tax dollars that would not exist if they choose to go somewhere else." But that's the key issue: Is it true that none of these jobs would have existed in the state but for the incentives? If three-fourths of the incented firms would have located in the state anyway, then those incentives are giving away tax dollars that state and local governments would have otherwise received.

THE DEVIL IS IN THE DETAILS

As discussion in this chapter shows, the benefits and costs of incentives for a state's residents are affected by many factors. In the next chapter, I report how these factors add up in determining benefits—and what difference is made by specific policies.

Chapter 4

Improving Incentives

What Can Policymakers Do?

As shown in Chapter 3, many factors affect incentive benefits. How do these all add up? What can policymakers do to increase the incentive benefit-cost ratio?

To begin, I present a baseline model of incentive benefits and costs. The baseline is not The Truth. As we will see, tweaking assumptions in the model can significantly change the benefit-cost ratio.

In this chapter, I use this baseline model for comparison purposes: can we significantly improve benefits by reforming incentives? I also use the baseline model to show how incentive benefits are typically distributed: How are the benefits of typical incentives distributed among different types of income, and across different income groups?

THE BASELINE MODEL

The baseline model, which I have described in detail elsewhere, reflects all the multipliers and spillovers, and leakages and negative cost feedbacks, described in Chapter 3.[58] The baseline model is a model of how a state economy works—how its labor market responds to various changes, how its housing market responds, how state and local government revenue and spending respond—and how all of this affects state job growth and the income per capita of state residents. The model uses estimates from research on the magnitude of all these factors in a state economy that might alter incentive benefits.

The baseline model makes the following assumptions:[59]

- The incentives analyzed are tax incentives or other cash incentives, not services. As mentioned in Chapter 2, cash incentives are over 90 percent of total incentives. The incentive program is an average state's incentive program, with incentives somewhat front-loaded in the first year, but continuing at a fairly high level through year 10, as shown in Figure 2.2. This incentive package is assumed to have a "but for" percentage of about 12 percent—the incentive package induces the location or expansion decision in 12 percent of the firms receiving incentives. For a typical incentive package, this is a plausible incentive effect.[60]

- The state's unemployment rate is assumed to be 3.9 percent, which was the U.S. average unemployment rate for 2018.[61]

- The effective job multiplier rate for the incented jobs, after including negative cost feedbacks, is assumed to be 1.75. In other words, for every 100 jobs directly created by incentives, a net of another 75 jobs are created in the state, resulting in 175 total jobs. As discussed in Chapter 3, such a state multiplier value would be typical for most jobs in a low-unemployment local economy. Higher multipliers will occur for high-tech industries in high-tech areas, or in high-unemployment areas; the effects of higher multipliers will be discussed later.[62]

- The incentive program, after allowing for fiscal benefits, is assumed to be paid for by increases in household taxes. This provides a good basis for comparison with other methods of financing incentives.

All these assumptions will be altered when I turn to considering different incentive policies.

This baseline model finds a benefit-cost ratio of 1.52.[63] Gross benefits are $1.52 per dollar of incentives costs, and net benefits are 0.52. Considering all effects on state residents' per capita incomes, for every dollar we put into incentives, per capita incomes ignoring incentives go up by $1.52. Including incentive costs, net per capita incomes go up by $0.52 per incentive dollar. These figures for benefits and costs are all calculated in what economists call present values: future benefits and costs are discounted to their equivalent in dollars today.[64]

So, incentives pass a benefit-cost test. They're the greatest thing since sliced bread. Let's charge right ahead and double current incentives from $50 billion to $100 billion.

Not necessarily. This 1.52 benefit-cost ratio is sensitive to various assumptions.

As just one example, suppose the "but for" percentage is lower. Suppose business location and expansion decisions are only half as sensitive to business costs as assumed in the baseline model. This would yield a "but for" percentage of around 6 percent. Such a lower "but for" percentage would be compatible with many research studies.[65]

With the halved "but for" percentage, the incentive benefit-cost ratio drops to 0.92. Benefits are now slightly less than incentive costs, so state residents lose, albeit slightly, from this typical incentive package.

My point: a 1.52 benefit-cost ratio is small enough that it doesn't leave much margin for less favorable assumptions, but assumptions that are still plausible.[66] Nor does it leave much room for variations in the benefit-cost ratio due to different state circumstances or different incentive program details.[67] We might not want to do a hard sell on expanding incentives unless we can find an incentive program design with a lot higher benefit-cost ratio than 1.52.

But back to the baseline model. The baseline model reveals some typical patterns in how incentive benefits are distributed.

Distribution across Income Types

First, consider how incentive benefits are distributed across different income types (Table 4.1). Fiscal benefits offset only about one-fifth of incentive costs. Under realistic assumptions, incentives rarely

Table 4.1 Types of Income Benefits for State Residents, as a Ratio to Incentive Costs

Earnings benefits	1.06
Property value benefits	0.34
Fiscal benefits	0.20
Losses to local business owners from higher costs	−0.08
Total gross benefits (sum of above 4 types)	1.52
Minus incentive costs	−1.00
Net income per capita increase for state residents	0.52

SOURCE: Author's calculations.

pay for themselves. Property value benefits are slightly higher, at about one-third of incentive costs. Property owners should be willing to pay a sizable chunk of the costs of incentive programs.[68]

But the main benefit of incentives is the resulting increase in per capita earnings. Incentives may have modest "but for" percentages and multiplier effects on boosting jobs. But more jobs are very valuable for a state's workers. Wage rates go up, as do employment rates.

Incentives should primarily be considered a labor market policy. Incentives boost labor demand. Incentives should be considered along with other labor demand and labor supply policies—public jobs programs, job training, etc.—in debates over how state and local governments can help workers. Which mix of policies will be the cheapest way to boost earnings prospects for different groups?

Why are the earnings benefits from incentives so much greater than other benefits, such as property value benefits or fiscal benefits? The relatively large size of earnings benefits is due in part to their persistence. In the short run, more local jobs help the local nonemployed get jobs. Crucially, these short-run effects persist. Short-run job experience boosts these workers' skills, and thereby their long-run earnings.

In contrast, the property value gain from a boost to local jobs is a one-time capital gain. Fiscal benefits are only a small fraction of the earnings gains from growth, as state and local governments tax only a portion of any increased income, and these tax revenue gains are offset mostly by increased public service needs from a larger population.[69]

Distribution across Income Groups

Second, consider how incentive benefits are distributed across different income groups. Incentives boost earnings mainly by boosting employment rates. Of the total earnings benefits in Table 4.1, over two-thirds is due to higher employment rates.[70] We would expect such employment rate increases to be the most valuable for lower-income groups, which have the lowest baseline employment rates.

In this baseline model, the progressive distribution of incentive benefits holds true (Figure 4.1). To look at income distribution effects, we first rank all households by household income, adjusted for the household's needs based on the number of persons in the household.[71]

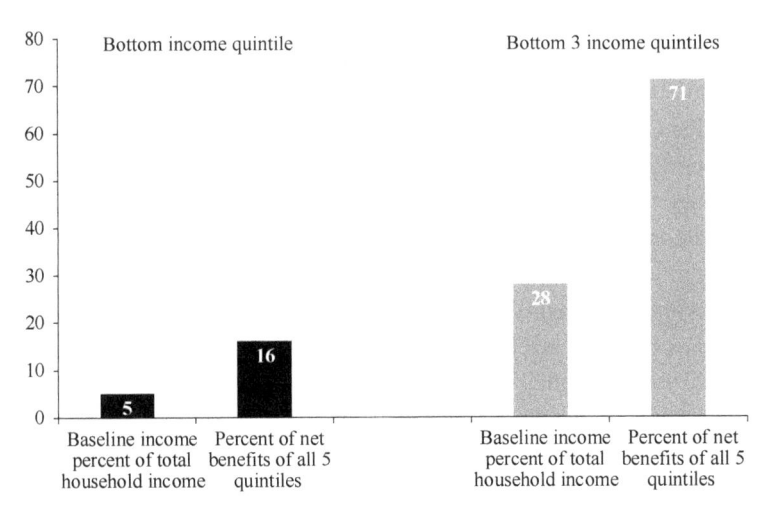

Figure 4.1 Baseline Income Shares vs. Share of Net Benefits

	Bottom income quintile	Bottom 3 income quintiles
Baseline income percent of total household income	5	28
Percent of net benefits of all 5 quintiles	16	71

NOTE: Sources and uses of income distribution data are given in more detail in Bartik (2018a). Note that percentages are of net benefits, that is, the net income figures subtract out what it costs each quintile to pay for the incentives, after fiscal benefits.
SOURCE: Author's calculations.

We then set income cutoffs to distribute households into five groups, each with the same number of persons. We look at the prevailing distribution of income across these five income quintiles to see what percentage each group usually receives of the total economic pie. We then look at what percentage each income quintile receives of the net income gains associated with incentives, to see if the percentage they receive differs from their usual share.[72]

For the households in the bottom one-fifth of the income distribution, in the prevailing income distribution, such low-income households have only 5 percent of total household income. But they receive 16 percent of the net benefits of incentives for household income. So, this moderately successful incentive program, with a benefit-cost ratio of 1.52, would tend to boost the lowest-income quintile's share of total household income. To put it another way, the percentage boost to income for this lowest-income quintile is triple the average for all households.

This progressivity also provides above-average benefits, in percentage terms, for the bottom three-fifths of the income distribution. In the baseline economy, the lowest three income quintiles get a little more than one quarter (28 percent) of the economic pie, yet they receive over two-thirds of the increase in net household income from incentives. Their percentage boost in income is more than twice the average for all households. Research suggests that these bottom- and middle-income groups gain the most from increases in local employment rates.[73]

Although incentives are progressive, this progressivity is moderate. For example, welfare and social programs might distribute close to 100 percent of their benefits to the lowest-income quintile. Expanding incentives would not be a substitute for expanding social programs. Financing incentives by cutting welfare programs would be unlikely to pay off for the lowest-income quintile.[74] Job creation does have progressive benefits, but its benefits are more broadly distributed than welfare benefits.

What is true is that incentive policy, and other labor demand policies—*if* they are successful, in that they have a benefit-cost ratio significantly greater than 1.0—tend to do two things: 1) disproportionately help the lowest income quintile, and 2) disproportionately help households up through the middle-income quintile. Incentives and other labor demand policies can be progressive, and yet help voters across a broad range of the income distribution. Politically, this is a big plus.

Many policy debates include discussion about "inclusive growth," by which is meant whether regional or national growth includes gains for all groups. Inclusive growth is a buzzword talked about by the World Bank,[75] the Brookings Institution,[76] and numerous foundations;[77] inclusive growth even has its own Wikipedia page.[78] What Figure 4.1 reveals is that policies that promote local job growth tend to be *modestly* inclusive. This inclusivity is because of local job growth to some extent increasing local employment rates in both the short run and long run. If local employment rates were unchanged by local job growth, then the main beneficiaries would be property owners; this would be "noninclusive growth."

The modest inclusivity of local job growth policies is not written in stone, impervious to policy design. Local job growth policies that target more jobs on the local nonemployed are more inclusive, and policies that target fewer jobs on the nonemployed are less inclusive. Furthermore, this modest inclusivity can be offset if the incentives policy is paid for too regressively; that is, it has much higher percentage costs for lower-income groups. Incentive financing is discussed later in this chapter.

WHY AVERAGE INCENTIVES HAVE BENEFITS CLOSE TO COSTS

This 1.52 estimated benefit-cost ratio for average incentives comes from a model. This model has been explained, but to most readers probably will still be a black box. The model has many moving parts; it can be hard to understand what generates the results. Can any intuition be provided for *why* average incentives have benefits close to costs?

Here's a back-of-the-envelope calculation that may be helpful to some readers. Average incentives are equivalent to providing incented firms with an incentive equal to 3 percent of their wage bill for 20 years. The "but for" is around 12 percent, so for the 12 percent of jobs that are created, the cost of creating jobs is about 25 percent of these jobs' wage bill (3 percent of the incented jobs divided by the 12 percent of incented jobs that are induced). If the average multiplier is 1.75, then the cost of creating total jobs will end up being reduced, by dividing by 1.75, to about 14 percent (= 25 percent / 1.75) of the wage bill of the total jobs created.[79] So, to summarize the cost side of the equation, average incentives, in the assumed low unemployment rate environment, will have a cost of around 14 percent of the wage bill of the total jobs, with multiplier, that are created. Incentives don't have to pay 100 percent of the wage bill to generate jobs, but they do have to pay a significant share.

On the benefits side, the main advantage is earnings benefits, which in turn is mostly due to higher employment rates. In a low-unemployment environment, the increase in the employment rate over time will average around 12 percent of the newly created jobs. So, the earnings benefits from higher employment rates in the state will average around 12 percent of the wage bill of the total jobs created. When one adds in more minor benefits (some wage increases, fiscal benefits, property value benefits), total benefits end up being modestly greater than total costs. Incentives' benefits are not close to being 100 percent of the new jobs' wage bill.

Of course, these different assumptions can be questioned. Perhaps the "but for" is higher, or the multiplier, or the percent of jobs going to local residents. But the baseline model uses estimates that are plausible, with backing research evidence. It is risky for policymakers to cherry-pick more favorable assumptions. Far better is reforming incentives to significantly increase the benefit-cost ratio. Modest improvements in the benefit-cost ratio are not enough if incentives are to play a significant role in improving state residents' well-being. There are alternatives to incentives that can do much better than a 1.52 benefit-cost ratio, as we will now discuss.

AVERAGE INCENTIVES ARE DOMINATED BY BETTER POLICIES

A big problem with the modest 1.52 benefit-cost ratio for average incentive policies: other policies can do more per dollar to boost state residents' incomes. What other policies? Expanded infrastructure and skills development programs, to name a couple.

Before discussing infrastructure and skills development programs, I want to provide a perspective on how to consider summary ratings of policies, such as cost per job or benefit-cost ratios. Such summary ratings deserve consideration in setting policy priorities. But they are not the only consideration.

You don't necessarily want to always exclusively choose the policy with the highest benefit-cost ratio, any more than you always want to choose the movie with the best Rotten Tomatoes Rating, and never see any movie with just "OK" reviews. Other considerations may affect your choice.

In the case of policy, other considerations include that different policies have different effects over time, and benefit somewhat different people. For example, some skills development programs, such as preschool education, have most benefits decades later. The job creation from incentives provides benefits immediately.[80] In addition, the job creation benefits from incentive programs may help a 55-year-old worker, who is unlikely to benefit from most job training programs.

However, benefit-cost ratios and cost per job should certainly be strongly considered in setting policy priorities. If BetterPolicy has a benefit-cost ratio that is twice as great as GoodPolicy, or a cost per job created that is half as much, a governor or mayor probably should avoid cutting funding on BetterPolicy as a way to fund GoodPolicy. Also, expanding funding for BetterPolicy will increase income per capita. With expanded income per capita, we can increase tax rates, and also choose to fund GoodPolicy and still have some income left over. So, if infrastructure and skills development programs can have higher benefit-cost ratios than average incentive policies, that is certainly an argument for prioritizing infrastructure and skills development policies in creating our state and local economic development policies. Let's start with expanding BetterPolicy, with its higher benefit-cost ratio, before going on to expand GoodPolicy.

Infrastructure

Infrastructure investment—roads, rail, water and sewer lines, energy hook-ups, communication networks, environmental clean-up, land development—has long been used to promote local economic development. From the Erie Canal to the transcontinental railroad to California water projects to the interstate highway system to brownfield cleanup to industrial parks, improving local infrastructure has helped attract and grow local jobs.

Public infrastructure leads to persistent boosts in jobs by lowering private costs. For example, highways lower transport costs for both businesses and households, making the area a more attractive location. As a result, private investment increases and new jobs are created. These new and better jobs develop the skills of local workers. These better skills and higher private investment lead to the area having persistent gains in more jobs and better jobs.

Federally funded economic development programs such as the Tennessee Valley Authority (TVA, most active from the 1930s through the 1950s) and the Appalachian Regional Commission (ARC, most active in the 1960s and 1970s) have spurred regional economic development with federal funding of better regional infrastructure. TVA invested in electrification, attracting many manufacturing jobs.

ARC invested in a regional highway system, which boosted job and income growth.

Based on research, infrastructure investment can be a cost-effective way to create jobs. Such investment can be more cost-effective than average incentives. Per job created, some infrastructure investment has been found to have less than one-fifth the costs of average incentives.[81]

Skills Development

Skills development programs—job training or education programs—can often be a cost-effective way to boost state residents' earnings per capita. They can have large and persistent effects on a person's earnings. Among those experiencing earnings gains, a sufficient proportion remain in the state for the skills investment to pay off for the state economy.

Skills development programs can have persistent effects on earnings because "skills beget skills," as Nobel Prize–winning economist James Heckman has said. Developing skills *now* leads to persons doing better in *later* education and training, and in *later* being more successful in getting better jobs, which further develop skills. Skills now, higher earnings for a lifetime.

From past studies of migration patterns, we know Americans are less hypermobile than people think. For example, over 60 percent of Americans spend most of their working career in the state in which they spent their early childhood.[82] Even among college graduates, at least 50 percent spend most of their career in their childhood state.

Consider high-quality preschool. Based on research, high-quality preschool will increase educational attainment and earnings over the entire career for former preschool participants. Most of these increased earnings don't begin to occur for at least 15 years—we're not sending former preschoolers into the workforce at age 5—but even so, the present value of the increase in career earnings is far greater than the cost of providing preschool. Suppose we count as benefits only the earnings gains of former preschool participants who stay in the same state. In the cost calculation for preschool, we include program costs for all preschool participants, including the one-third or more who will move out of state. But we throw away in our benefit calculations the earnings gains for those persons who participate in preschool in Michigan and end up for some reasons moving as an adult to Ohio. Despite throwing away these benefits for out-migrants, a high-quality preschool program can boost the present value of the increase in per capita earnings, for persons who stay in the same state, by over 5 times the program costs for all preschool participants.

Other well-designed skills development programs also can have high ratios of earnings benefits to costs (Figure 4.2).[83] These benefit-to-cost calculations are from a state perspective: we look only at the increase in future earnings of persons who stay in the same state. Community college workforce programs can have a ratio of earnings benefits in the state, to costs, of over 8-to-1. Increases in public school

Figure 4.2 Benefit-Cost Ratios for Alternative State Policies

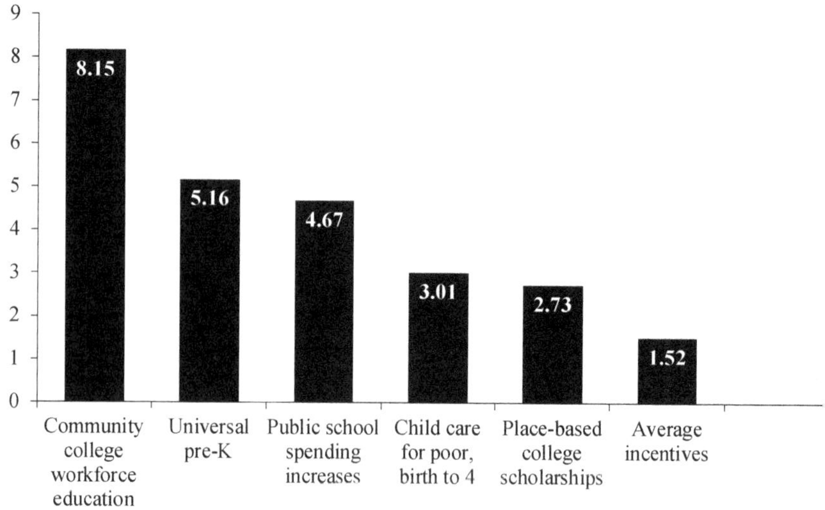

Community college workforce education	8.15
Universal pre-K	5.16
Public school spending increases	4.67
Child care for poor, birth to 4	3.01
Place-based college scholarships	2.73
Average incentives	1.52

SOURCE: Author's calculations.

spending can have earnings benefits-to-cost ratios from a state perspective of almost 5-to-1. High-quality child care can have earnings benefit-to-cost ratios from a state perspective of about 3-to-1. Place-based scholarship programs award college scholarships broadly to persons in a particular community and/or graduating from a particular high school, usually restricted to colleges in that state. These programs can have earnings benefits-to-cost ratios from a state resident perspective of a little under 3-to-1.

Multiple skills programs can increase state per capita earnings by three to eight times their costs. Average incentives increase state per capita earnings by less than twice their costs. If states have additional revenues, governors and legislators should put a higher priority on fully funding these high-quality skills programs, not additional incentives, at least if those incentives are typically designed incentives.

Opportunity Costs of Financing Incentives with School Spending Cuts

A big concern is whether incentives in practice are financed by reducing spending on programs that are more effective in boosting state residents' earnings per capita. This concern is most acute for K–12 spending. As discussed in Chapter 2, over one-quarter of incentives are property tax abatements, which reduce normal property tax collections. Given the reliance of public schools on property tax revenue, property tax abatements may often lead to some downward pressures on school budgets. States also spend a great deal on K–12, on average about one-sixth of state general expenditures. State incentives might sometimes impinge on state aid to local public schools.

If an average incentive package is paid for by reducing K–12 spending—that is, without the property tax abatements and state tax credits, K–12 spending would have been higher by that incentive amount—then the benefits versus costs of incentives dramatically change. The benefit-cost ratio of this average incentive policy becomes *minus* 3.77. For each dollar devoted to incentives, state residents' incomes are reduced by $3.77—and once we account for the dollar cost of incentives, income per capita is reduced by $4.77 per dollar of incentives.

Under this scenario, the incentives still create jobs in the short run. These short-run jobs have some short-run benefits for boosting state residents' incomes. But these incentives must be paid for. If paid for by reducing public school spending, these spending cuts undermine the quality of public schools. The lower quality translates into lower future earnings per capita. High school dropout rates may go up, and college attendance and graduation may go down, which will lower earnings. Among students whose educational attainment is unchanged, the lower public school quality may lower their skills, which will also lower earnings. In the model, these lower earnings are counted only for public school students who stay in the state. Counting out-migrants to other states, the full earnings loss is higher.

The lower earnings due to lower school spending occurs mostly in the long run. We pay for incentives in the short run. These spending cuts lower the quality of public schools now. But the effects of a school's lower quality on earnings won't become large for at least 20 or 30 years, when former public school students reach their peak earnings years.

In the model, poorly financed incentives—paid for by lower public school spending—still have net benefits for state residents for 21 years. But after that, net benefits become net costs. The negative effects of cutting school funding end up causing considerable fiscal costs for state and local governments, which must be paid for, and put additional downward pressure on public school funding. The policy causes the state economy to enter a dangerous downward spiral, as public school funding cuts lead to lower earnings, which lowers state revenue, which leads to further school funding cuts.

Financing incentives via public school spending cuts is not only bad for the overall state economy but also has disproportionate costs for lower-income groups. Better public school quality tends to have broad benefits. All income groups have children who benefit from higher public school quality, due in part to higher future earnings. Because lower-income groups tend to have children with lower predicted future earnings, any cuts in public school quality have larger percentage costs for lower-income groups.[84] In the model, financing incentives by cuts in public school spending has negative percentage effects on all income groups, but these percentage losses are far greater for the lowest-income households, the households in the lowest-income quintile. For the lowest-income quintile, the percentage loss is over four times as great as the average household's loss.

Assuming 100 percent of incentive costs are financed by K–12 spending cuts is an extreme assumption. But incentives have net costs under less extreme assumptions. Based on some experimentation with the model, net incentive benefits turn negative as the share of incentives financed by K–12 spending cuts increases from 11 percent to 12 percent.

High-Quality Public Infrastructure and Skills Development Programs versus Average Incentives

Will every infrastructure project create jobs at one-fifth the cost of incentives? No. Will every skills development program have earnings benefits of three to eight times its costs? No.

Infrastructure projects can be boondoggles. An infrastructure project can be a bridge to nowhere. Infrastructure costs can be pushed up by cost-plus contracts, project delays and redesigns due to undue regulatory reviews, and excessive staffing requirements.

Not every skills development program will develop the needed skills. A preschool may fail to achieve good results if it has high teacher turnover and poorly trained teachers. A community college worker training program may miss the mark if the college staff are not attuned to the latest job requirements.

Quality matters. My comparisons so far in this chapter may have been unfair to incentives by comparing *average* incentives with well-designed infrastructure and skills development programs, and further assuming that these good designs are well implemented.

However, these comparisons do show that average-quality incentives have good alternatives: investing in high-quality infrastructure and skills development programs. Governors and mayors, in making budget choices to advance state and local economic development, should prioritize high-quality public infrastructure and skills development programs over average incentives.

BETTER INCENTIVE POLICIES

But our incentives don't have to be average. Better policies can improve incentives' multipliers and spillovers and reduce leakages and negative feedbacks. I now consider various policy changes to reform incentives. Unless otherwise specified, each policy change is undertaken separately, with all other factors staying the same. Table 4.2 summarizes how each policy change affects the incentive policy's benefit-cost ratio.

Increasing Effects on Incented Firms

Incentives can be improved by policies that increase their impact on incented firms, per dollar of incentives. Tax incentives can be made more cost-effective by making more of the incentive payments up front. The corporate executives deciding on whether to open a new plant or expand an existing plant are focused on the short term. Eliminating incentives that are 10 years out and making those payments up front would have greater effects on location and expansion decisions, per dollar of cost to the government.[85] The model estimates that this increases job creation effects per dollar by about 38 percent. Making all incentives up front increases the benefit-cost ratio from 1.52 to 2.13.[86]

Up-front incentives face the challenge of what to do if the firm leaves sooner than expected. Compared to the usual incentive package, an up-front package will have already paid out more dollars if the

Table 4.2 Benefit-Cost Ratios of Alternative Incentive Policies

Type of policy reform	Description	Benefit-cost ratio
Baseline	Average incentive policy in low-unemployment area, not targeted on high-tech cluster, financed by household taxes	1.52
Increase effects per $ on incented firms	Up-front incentives	2.13
	Business services	16.15
Increase multiplier	High-tech cluster	2.71
	Locally owned incented firms	2.51
Increase local worker hiring	High-unemployment area	3.15
	Job training services	2.03
Alternative financing mechanisms for incentive costs	Cut K–12	−3.77
	Higher business taxes	1.90

NOTE: See text and endnotes for assumptions made. Each policy reform changes one feature of incentive design.
SOURCE: Author's calculations.

firm unexpectedly leaves. This challenge can be addressed by including clawback provisions in the incentive contract. The clawback provisions would specify repayments if the firm leaves early.

More dramatic increases in the benefit-cost ratio are possible with high-quality customized business services. As already mentioned, research suggests that, compared to handing firms tax incentives and other cash services, customized services' effects per dollar on job creation are 10 times greater. A manufacturing extension service that gives a smaller manufacturer some good advice on targeting new markets may have large effects on the manufacturer's competitiveness, yet the advice is relatively cheap to provide. A community college that does a great job of providing skilled workers to local firms may persistently improve their competitiveness by far more than a one-time cash grant of the same cost. In addition, such customized services are up-front assistance, which is more salient to business decision makers.

Such high-quality customized business services have a benefit-cost ratio for state residents of over 16-to-1. Intuitively, the benefit-cost ratio of these up-front services increases by about 10 times what occurs with baseline tax incentives.[87] The local job creation helps state residents a lot, compared to these services' modest costs.

The limitation policymakers face is that these customized services are useful only to a limited clientele of mostly smaller firms that are expanding and can use such services. Furthermore, achieving such high benefit-cost ratios requires that the government maintain these services' high quality. Scaling up customized services is more challenging than scaling up tax incentives. The government can easily scale up tax and other cash incentives. Cash is valued by all firms and is easy to hand out.

Increasing Multipliers

Incentives' benefits can improve if we increase multiplier effects on the state's total jobs. Multipliers can be increased by targeting high-tech firms in cities with high-tech clusters. As discussed in the previous chapter, these higher multipliers for high tech will occur only in the 60 or so cities with the greatest concentration of high tech. In these 60 high-tech areas, each new job in a high-tech firm might increase total jobs in the state by three (the high-tech job plus two other jobs), up from the 1.7–2.0 multiplier range for more typical industries in more typical areas. With such higher multipliers, incentives' benefit-cost ratio increases from 1.52 to 2.71.

Multipliers can also be increased by targeting firms with local owners, who are more likely to use local suppliers, and who also personally spend more locally. In addition to modestly increasing the multiplier, local ownership also means that the incentives increase the income of local residents, not out-of-state owners. Local ownership increases incentives' benefit-cost ratio to 2.51.[88]

Increasing State Residents' Share of the New Jobs

Incentives' benefits will improve if more jobs go to state residents who otherwise would not be employed. This job share will increase significantly if incentives are targeted at local labor markets (metropolitan areas or similar areas within which people commute to work) that have high rates of nonemployment. In addition to increasing the share of jobs that go to the local nonemployed, the greater availability of local labor supply will increase the job multiplier. Targeting a local economy with unemployment of 10 percent, rather than the baseline model's assumed unemployment of 3.9 percent, increases the benefit-cost ratio for incentives from 1.52 to 3.15.[89]

More jobs will also go to the local nonemployed if state policy seeks to encourage firms to do such hiring. For example, if the local job training agency does a good job of identifying and training the local nonemployed for available job openings, the share of new jobs that go to local residents will go up. If at least a portion of incentives come in the form of customized job training services, such hiring of the local nonemployed may be encouraged by the incentive package. The baseline initial percentage of new jobs that go to the local nonemployed is around 55 percent. Suppose we assume that providing high-quality job training services for filling new jobs could increase this percentage by a factor of 1.50, to a little over 82 percent of all new jobs being filled by the local nonemployed. Then the benefit-cost ratio for incentives increases to 2.03.

Why can't more effective job training do as much to improve incentives' benefits as targeting high-unemployment areas? Based on empirical studies of how new jobs are filled, in a local area with unemployment of 10 percent, over 97 percent of new jobs in the short run will be filled by local residents who otherwise would be nonemployed. In a local economy with 3.9 percent unemployment, it seems implausible that local job training policy could reach 97 percent.[90] In addition, local economies with high nonemployment will have higher local job multipliers because of the greater effective labor supply.[91]

Financing Incentives with Fewer State Resident Burdens

As already mentioned, the baseline model assumes that incentives are financed by higher taxes on households. As shown, if we further burden local residents by financing incentives by cuts in public school spending, the benefit-cost ratio for incentives changes from the baseline 1.52 to −3.77.

The financial burden of incentives on state residents can be reduced by financing incentives with higher overall business tax rates. In the model, higher business tax rates have two contradictory effects. On the one hand, higher business taxes reduce some private investment and job growth in the state. On the other hand, higher business taxes export some of the financial burden of paying for incentives to business owners who live out of state. Which dominates?

The model suggests that, on net, the advantage to exporting business taxes to out-of-state business owners outweighs depressing effects on business investment. The benefit-cost ratio for incentives increases to 1.90.

Why do incentives dominate lower business taxes in increasing a state's private sector job growth? As discussed in Chapter 3, incentives are better targeted than lower business taxes, in two ways. The first way is that incentives are targeted at tradable goods and services, and jobs in these industries have greater effects on boosting local economic growth. The second way is that incentives are targeting firms that are making investment and job creation decisions. Business tax cuts go to many firms that aren't even thinking about expanding in the state.

Synergistic Effects

Of course, policymakers can pursue several policy reforms to incentives at the same time. Such simultaneous reforms tend to have synergistic, multiplicative effects. Increasing multipliers or the jobs going to state residents has a multiplied effect if combined with more cost-effective business services. The greater initial jobs per dollar then yield multiplied greater benefits by being multiplied by a greater job multiplier or a greater job share going to local residents.

For example, cost-effective business services by themselves have a benefit-cost ratio of 16.15. When combined with targeting high-tech firms in a high-tech cluster area, the ratio increases to 28.07. When cost-effective business services are targeted at a high-unemployment local labor market, the benefit-cost ratio increases to 33.02.

Making a Difference with Incentives

For incentives to truly make a difference for state residents, incentives need to have a sizable benefit-cost ratio. Otherwise, incentives will always have too small benefits to really be more than a rounding error in a large state economy. If incentives' benefit-cost ratio is modest, there are better ways of helping boost state residents' income per capita.

Average incentives have too many leakages, and too small multipliers, to have large benefits relative to costs. Reforming incentives to improve benefit-cost ratios requires finding the key leverage points, where a modest change in incentive policy can yield significant effects for a much larger state economy.

A key leverage point is putting limits on tax incentives that are too general, which go to all areas and all tradable firms. Incentives should be more targeted, either on high unemployment areas, or on high-tech firms in high-tech areas. Some of the savings from limiting untargeted tax incentives could be used to address another leverage point: expanding high-quality services to smaller businesses. Other savings could be used to expand nonincentive policies to improve earnings, such as high-quality skills development programs. In addition, limiting the overall incentive budget would reduce the odds that incentives end up impinging on public services that promote economic development, such as public schools or roads.

These reforms are much more likely if we have better techniques of evaluating incentives, so that policymakers are encouraged to modify the targeting and design of incentives to be more effective. In the next chapter, I turn to the incentive evaluation challenge.

Chapter 5
Are My State's Incentives Working?

Practical Evaluation Strategies for Incentive Programs

As shown in prior chapters, research around the nation suggests what incentive designs work best. But are my state's incentives working? This question is asked by state policymakers and voters.

In recent years, state evaluation of incentive programs has increased.[92] Thirty-one states now mandate that their incentive programs be evaluated on some timetable.[93] What advice on doing such evaluations can be given to state analysts?

My opening advice: avoid reinventing the wheel. We already know a lot about incentives, as described in prior chapters. Sometimes, state evaluators can provide governors and legislators with useful information by adapting these national research results to a particular state incentive program.

In addition, the evaluation doesn't have to use the latest econometrics. Useful information can come from surveys.

USE A MODEL

Evaluations should do more than estimate the causal effects of incentives on job creation by incented firms. Incentives are only justified if they benefit state residents. These benefits include effects on state residents' per capita incomes. To see how per capita incomes in a state are affected by job creation in incented firms requires a model. Such a model, which was outlined in the prior chapters in this book, should describe how the state's economy, labor market, tax revenue, and spending needs respond to incented firms' job increases.

To summarize, here are the key elements that must be present in a reasonable incentive impact model:

- An estimate of the job impact of incentives on firms receiving them
- The state job multiplier of the incented jobs
- What proportion of the total new jobs, after the multiplier, will go to state residents vs. in-migrants, and how this varies with local economic conditions
- How job growth and population growth affect state and local tax revenue and public spending needs
- If the incentive is financed by cutting public spending that affects the state economy's productivity, an estimate of the economic impact of this spending cut

Where do states get such a model? Ideally a state would already have some econometric model of the state economy and labor market. This model should be able to estimate the multiplier and what proportion of jobs go to state residents vs. in-migrants. A state econometric model could also be adapted to plug in plausible productivity effects from spending cuts. States should also have a fiscal impact model; this fiscal impact model should make realistic assumptions about how growth affects spending needs for infrastructure and public services.

Not every model will be suitable, at least without some adjustments. For example, as discussed in Chapter 4, commonly used models overstate the multiplier by at least one-third. Evaluators might want to adjust some models' multipliers downward by one-third.[94]

Alternatively, a state could use some of the parameters outlined in prior chapters to get back-of-the-envelope calculations of plausible effects of job growth on multipliers, earnings per capita, and the state fiscal situation. Or the state could adapt the model underlying Chapter 4, which is based on a generic state, to its own circumstances.

But all of this starts with how the incentive affected incented jobs. How can a state's evaluators determine reasonable estimates of these effects? What is the "but for" of state tax incentives? How much does it cost in customized business services to create one job?

EVALUATING JOB CREATION EFFECTS ON INCENTED FIRMS: THE SELECTION BIAS CHALLENGE

A state's evaluators might have some data on job creation in incented firms, or on how many incented jobs are created in each of the state's counties. How can an evaluator determine what percentage of these incented jobs are a result of the incentives, the "but for" percentage? To do so, the evaluator must have some basis for comparison—some estimate of what would have happened in a hypothetical world without the incentives, to be able to see what the incentives have done. This is hard to do. As statisticians and econometricians will annoyingly point out, many evaluations are likely to yield estimates of incentive effects that are biased.

The challenge is that the incented firms and areas are not randomly chosen, but rather for some reason are selected to receive incentives. That reason for selection may have its own effects on job growth, and bias estimates of the incentives, leading to selection bias. There is self-selection bias: firms decided to apply for incentives, or more firms in certain areas applied for incentives, or the area decided to push incentives more. There is program selection bias: economic development agencies for some reason selected these firms or areas.

Incentives often by design are disproportionately awarded to new or expanding firms. If our basis for comparison is all firms, we would expect firms receiving incentives to be more likely to expand, given that expansion is a criterion for selection. This is positive selection bias: even if incentives had no effect, incented firms would be more likely to expand.

On the other hand, suppose we switch the comparison group to all firms that expand. In that case, out of all firms that expand, perhaps firms that have more challenges are more likely to apply for incentives or more likely to be awarded incentives. This is negative selection bias: even if incentives had no true effect, incented firms might, because of their greater challenges, tend to grow by a smaller percentage.

Incentives for job retention might also have either negative or positive selection bias. Compared to all firms, firms receiving job retention incentives might be less likely to do well, as they were selected because they were at risk of job loss, resulting in negative selection bias. On the other hand, compared to other firms that have a recent history of job loss, firms receiving job retention incentives would be those that selected not to make job cutbacks. This leads to positive selection bias: the factors that led the firm to not make job cutbacks might cause the incentives rather than the incentive causing the job retention.

Similar selection biases might occur in comparing counties with many incented jobs to counties with fewer incented jobs. Positive selection bias might occur because counties that grow faster will have more new or expanding firms, which will be more likely to receive incentives. On the other hand, negative selection bias might occur if the state's incentives target more troubled industries or counties. The challenge is that it is difficult to distinguish the true effects of incentives from the effects on county job growth of what types of firms, industries, or areas are selected for incentives.

OVERCOMING SELECTION BIAS

The perfect incentive evaluation: first, get hold of a time machine. Go back in time and eliminate the incentives. Return to the present and see how the world differs. Such a parallel worlds evaluation would tell us how each firm, county, or person is affected by incentives vs. no incentives.

Randomized Control Trials

A time machine isn't always around when you need one, so in its absence, incentives would ideally be evaluated via a randomized control trial. Firms or counties would be randomly assigned to either receive incentives or not receive incentives. Random assignment assures that we would expect the treatment group—the incented firms or counties—and the control group—the nonincented firms or counties—to have the same values of both observed and unobserved characteristics *on average*. As the sample size of firms or counties gets larger, this expectation of similar values of both observable and unobservable variables is increasingly likely to be realized in the observed sample, on average. Therefore, as sample size goes up, it is increasingly likely that any differences between the treatment group and the control group are due to the incentives, not other variables. The randomized control trial is increasingly likely to reveal the incentives' *average* effects.

In my view, randomized control trials by any individual state to evaluate incentives are likely to be rare.[95] States believe they can pick the firms or counties in which incentives will be more effective. Randomization eliminates the state's ability to pick the right firms or counties. Incentives also are meant to be perceived by firms as attractive. Being randomly assigned to a control group is off-putting.[96]

Quasi-Experiments

One alternative to a randomized experiment is a quasi-experiment, which indicates a situation where a firm or county receiving more incentives is due to factors that, on their own, would not be expected to affect job growth. If this is so, the observed association between incentives and job growth will reflect incentives' true causal effects. These quasi-experiments are of two types: natural experiments and designed quasi-experiments.

Natural Experiments

Sometimes, we are in luck: a quasi-experiment may arise naturally. A natural experiment is where access to the program just happens to be limited in a way that is not directly correlated with job growth. For example, access to an incentive program may vary with where the firm is located vs. the office delivering the program, or when in the program year the firm happens to apply. If these location or timing factors do not have strong job growth effects in their own right, the variation in incentive use that is correlated with location or time may reveal incentives' effects. Or there might be some quirk in program eligibility rules that leads to otherwise similar firms differing in their eligibility for a particular incentive. For example, some firms might be ineligible for a tax incentive program because they have no remaining business tax liability against which the tax incentive can be credited, or because the state has some cap on how much in incentives a firm can receive. Or a geographically targeted program might be awarded only to a subset of similar eligible areas, and the research evidence suggests that prior levels and trends of job growth are similar between the successful and unsuccessful applicant areas.

These examples are not hypothetical. Such evaluations sometimes have been possible:

- Manufacturing extension services have been evaluated by comparing firms receiving such services with otherwise similar firms that were less likely to receive services because they happened to be located farther away from the extension program office. This evaluation implies job creation effects per dollar of 10 times that of the average tax incentive.[97]

- Customized job training programs have been evaluated by comparing firms receiving training assistance with similar firms that applied late in the fiscal year, after training funds were exhausted. This evaluation suggests that such training services have job creation effects per dollar of 10 times that of the average tax incentive.[98]

- R&D tax credits have been evaluated by comparing firms receiving such credits with otherwise similar firms that were ineligible for additional R&D credits because they had exhausted their state tax liability or reached a cap on the maximum R&D credits received per firm.[99]
- The largest-ever federal regional economic development program, the Tennessee Valley Authority (TVA) program started in the 1930s, has been evaluated by comparing the assisted counties with counties in similar regions that were unsuccessfully proposed for similar regional development program assistance, which was mostly in the form of infrastructure funding. This evaluation found that TVA was cost-effective in creating manufacturing jobs. These manufacturing jobs in the TVA region have mostly persisted to the present, many years after the TVA's infrastructure investments were made.[100]

These evaluations have achieved reasonably precise and credible estimates of incentive effects. (See Box 5.1 for more on the R&D credit example.)

Two limitations should be noted. First, for some programs, sample sizes may be insufficient to detect the likely program effects. This problem depends in part on the sample sizes: how many firms receive incentives or how many geographic areas are targeted for economic development programs, and how many similar unassisted firms or geographic areas are available for comparison. This problem also depends in part on the likely program effects. For any given sample size, larger program effects on assisted firms or geographic areas are easier to detect.

Second, note that the existence of these credible comparison groups—firms or geographic areas that are similar to those receiving incentives but do not receive incentives—depends on the program being run at less than full scale. Only serving some eligible firms, or some eligible counties, would probably be common during a program's early years. So natural experiments may be feasible early on

> **Box 5.1 Evaluation of the Washington State High Technology Tax Credit**
>
> Begun in 1994, the state of Washington's high-technology tax credit provided a modest subsidy for R&D spending. The credit was limited to R&D spending above typical shares of a firm's gross receipts, and the credit was no more than 1.8 percent of such above-average R&D spending, with the credit varying by industry, firm circumstances, and over time. The state annually spent $20–$30 million on the credit. Average credits were $48,000 per firm. Around 500–600 firms annually received the credit, with the average firm having 250 employees. Half of assisted firms were in the professional, scientific, and technical services sector; 20 percent were in manufacturing.
>
> Using data on firms receiving the credit from 2004 to 2009, a 2012 evaluation exploited an aspect of the credit that was a natural experiment. First, the credit rate changed for some industries. Second, credits varied over time due to a firm's tax situation. The credit was nonrefundable, so a firm could not receive a credit if it had no state business taxes. In addition, the credit was capped at $2 million per firm.
>
> The evaluation found a statistically significant effect of credits on a firm's job growth. It took $55,000 in annual credit costs to create one job for one year.
>
> It is unlikely that one job created for one year yields benefits to Washington State residents that exceed $55,000. Only a portion of new jobs raise the employment-to-population ratio, so new jobs have benefits less than the wages paid.
>
> Based on the findings that the credit was relatively high cost, compared to its likely benefits, the state of Washington allowed this tax credit to expire in 2015.
>
> SOURCE: Bartik and Hollenbeck (2012).

in a program's history, when they would arguably be most useful. But as the program matures and is expanded to full scale, natural experiments may be less feasible. By then, we might hope a natural experiment evaluation has already been done.

For example, more recent studies of manufacturing extension services have been unable to find a significant effect of the firm's location versus the nearest extension office on the probability of the firm receiving services.[101] Apparently, manufacturing extension programs in the United States have succeeded in setting up a sufficient number of offices, and have advertised their services sufficiently that geographic access is no longer a big barrier to receiving services. This is good for program access and program impact, but bad for program evaluation. Luckily, in the case of manufacturing extension, an earlier evaluation study had already been done, back when the program's geographic access had determined which firms were served.

Evaluators cannot count on being lucky. Evaluators should look out for possible natural experiments (see Box 5.2), but they cannot be counted on to be there when needed to evaluate a specific incentive program. When natural experiments do occur, they are more likely in early program years.

Box 5.2 Questions to See If a Natural Experiment Evaluation Is Feasible

- Are there unassisted firms or geographic areas that are similar to those receiving economic development assistance?
- Can we explain why some firms or geographic areas received assistance from this program and others did not?
- Is it plausible that the factors explaining who is assisted do not directly affect the economic performance of a firm or geographic area?
- Does the program plausibly have large enough effects on economic performance for its impact to be statistically detected, given the sample size of those assisted vs. unassisted?

Designed Quasi-Experiments

But a quasi-experiment may arise deliberately, from program design. An incentives program can be deliberately designed to help create a good comparison group for assisted firms or counties.

For example, in choosing which firms receive tax incentives or customized services, a state can base this choice on a quantitative scoring system. This scoring system can accommodate whatever factors the state wants to consider in targeting incentives: likely state benefits from the incentive, whether the firm needs the incentive, and so on. Firms just above the cutoff may receive incentives, while those just below do not. Or firms just above the cutoff may receive much higher levels of incentives than those below the cutoff. The key is that firms just above or below the cutoff have large differences in incentives received, but firms just above or just below the cutoff are likely to be similar on observed and unobserved variables affecting job growth, other than the incentives' receipt. As a result, any observed differences between firms just above or below the cutoff are plausible estimates of incentives' true causal effects.

A similar planned quasi-experiment can be used to create a good comparison group for counties (or other geographic areas) that receive more incentives. A state could create different tiers of incentive eligibility for different geographic areas. For example, North Carolina annually ranks its 100 counties by measures of economic distress and divides them into three tiers; each tier has different eligibility for state incentives. Counties just above or below the cutoff for receiving a higher level of incentives should on average be similar in all observed and unobserved variables affecting county job growth, but for the incentive levels. The observed differences in county job growth between counties just above or below the cutoff are defensible estimates of how incentives affect a county's growth.

Among economists, such designed quasi-experiments go under the label "regression-discontinuity design," or RDD for short. Why this name? A regression is used to predict how the dependent variable, in this case job growth, varies continuously with some score used to determine eligibility for a program. We then incorporate the break or discontinuity at some score cutoff in eligibility for the program's treatment, in this case incentives, to identify the causal effects of the treatment.

RDD has been widely used in program evaluations, although *not* for incentive programs. For example, it has been used to estimate the effects of preschool programs on kindergarten entry test scores.[102] RDD has been shown to give estimates whose quantitative magnitudes are similar to randomized control trials.[103]

So, RDD can be a great econometric technique. Maybe incentive evaluators should catch up with the rest of the program evaluation field and use RDD extensively in incentive evaluation? Not so fast. For incentives, RDD at the state level has problems with desirability, precision, and availability. The desirability issues are most severe for RDD with individual firm data, the precision issue is most severe for RDD with geographic areas, and the availability problem often makes RDD impossible.

First, on the desirability issue: consider tax incentives to firms. Should we have a quantitative scoring system that causes a large, discrete change in tax incentive receipt or magnitude for firms above or below some cutoff score? My answer is no. If a firm is

- in a tradable industry; and
- is creating jobs in a geographic area with high social benefits from more jobs, such as a distressed area;

then tax incentive policy should encourage job creation in all such firms. Social benefits will occur from all such job creation. Perhaps social benefits may vary continuously across these firms. So, perhaps one should continuously vary the tax incentive with the firm's wages, job multiplier, or investment per job. But the rationale for a large, discrete jump in tax incentive magnitude is lacking. Such a jump helps evaluation but does not make sense for how tax incentives to firms should be awarded. This big jump in incentives, with a weak rationale, is particularly problematic because the incentives may give a significant competitive advantage to some firms over others. Unequal treatment by the government demands a compelling rationale.

Consider customized services to firms. For these services, considerable selectivity in who receives services is desirable. Advice is not equally useful to all firms. For example, some manufacturing firms have problems with the technology they use, or how they market their products, that can be readily addressed with good advice, whereas other manufacturing firms may not have such problems.

However, which firms are likely to benefit from customized services is hard to capture with a quantitative score. Say you're a staff person for a manufacturing extension service. How are you supposed to assign a quantitative score for "how much this firm needs advice" to each local manufacturer? The idea is absurd.

Consider targeting distressed counties. Should we have a quantitative scoring system that causes a large, discrete change in economic development programs for counties above or below some cutoff score? My answer is yes: not only will this help facilitate more rigorous evaluations, but it makes sense as a way for states to manage local economic development assistance.

The level of economic need may vary continuously across counties. Deciding which counties to target is to some extent arbitrary. But targeting a tier of distressed counties has great symbolic value: such an aim clearly communicates expectations to the voters and the private sector. In the absence of some arbitrary cutoff for helping distressed counties, it will be difficult for the public to hold policymakers accountable for targeting, and it will be difficult for the private sector to understand the state's targets. By targeting a most needy set of counties, the state can clearly show that it is committed to helping reduce the job shortage in these areas, and voters and the private sector can respond.

With better information on what areas are being targeted, the private sector is more likely to make investment decisions that favor distressed counties. The voters are better able to judge whether the state government's plans to help these distressed counties have worked. Continuous variation in economic development assistance across counties is more confusing than a clear target group.

Second, an RDD for geographic areas in a single state is likely to have some problems of imprecision. An RDD is less precise in estimating impacts than a randomized control trial. To achieve the same level of statistical significance as a randomized control trial, an RDD would need a sample size at least 2.5 times as large.[104]

The intuition for this discrepancy is as follows: a randomized control trial would determine who received the "treatment"—which in this case is the incentive—by random chance, flipping a coin. An RDD must infer from the data, using a regression, how a firm's or county's job growth is affected as one approaches the eligibility cutoff for the incentive, from either side. This extra inference requirement adds some extra statistical noise or uncertainty to the analysis. A larger sample size is needed to overcome this extra uncertainty.

This is a problem because there is a lot of statistical noise in job growth for individual firms or counties anyway. By statistical noise, I simply mean that there are many unobserved or even unobservable variables that help determine whether a given firm or county prospers or fails. A firm may happen to get a new contract, a county may happen to attract a growing firm. There's a lot of variety in economic development fortunes that we don't fully understand. Variety may be the spice of life, but this spice makes it more difficult to get good statistical precision in estimating the effects of incentives, or indeed any other variable, on firm or county job growth.

So, we may need to have large numbers of assisted and unassisted firms, or assisted and unassisted geographic areas, to get good precision in the estimated effects of tax incentives or customized services. Such large sample sizes might frequently be feasible with data for individual firms.

In the case of counties, the situation is worse. Most states don't have hundreds of counties. A single state analysis with cutoffs for incentive tiers will often give imprecise estimates of how incentives affect county job growth.

Geographic areas with cutoffs are more likely to have adequate sample sizes with a national sample of counties or other geographic areas. But this is only relevant for evaluations done at the national level of incentives, which is a separate topic, to be considered in a later chapter. Here we are focused on advice to give state evaluators.

These imprecision problems will not always prevent state RDD evaluations of economic development programs. If the program's expected effects are large enough, then even if the RDD estimates are somewhat imprecise, it still may be possible to estimate whether program effects are statistically significantly greater than whatever standard is set for the program being successful. For example, if a geographically targeted economic development program really makes a large difference to some geographic area's job growth, the statistical noise in area growth may not prevent an RDD evaluation of this geographic assistance (see Box 5.3 and Figure 5.1 for an example).

Third, from the viewpoint of a state analyst, the relevant issue is often how to evaluate incentives with the data at hand. Unless the analyst has the good fortune that some incentive program has been run with active use of a scoring cutoff, with adequate sample size, this entire discussion is irrelevant.

An economist can recommend use of RDD all he wants. But if the state's programs haven't been designed that way, or the sample size is low, the economist's recommendation is no more useful than the joke about the economist's advice about how to open a can without a can opener: "First, assume you have a can opener." If the can contains rigorous evaluation results, assuming that the RDD can opener is available does not magically provide a way to open the can and get the results.

Box 5.4 summarizes the questions that must be asked before planning an RDD of an economic development program. If all the answers are "Yes," then move forward with an RDD—if you can get a can opener, you don't need to assume one.

My guess: hell will be converted into a free hockey rink for the Detroit Red Wings before the average state will use a quantitative

Are My State's Incentives Working? 75

Box 5.3 A Regression-Discontinuity Design County Example with Hypothetical Program Effects

To illustrate the potential—and limits—of RDD, consider the following hypothetical program. We rank the 83 counties of Michigan by a distress indicator: the county's employment-to-population ratio in 2007. We imagine that in 2007, an economic development program began to assist 60 of these 83 counties. These 60 have the lowest 2007 employment rate, with 60 being the minimum number that comprise half of Michigan's population. The other 23 counties are unassisted.

These 60 distressed counties have employment rates of 50.6 percent or lower. As the county breakdown suggests, the distressed counties have lower average population than the other counties. The state's overall 2007 employment rate was 54.6 percent.

Suppose this hypothetical program increases average annual job growth, from 2007 to 2017, by 2 percentage points. Can RDD detect this effect?

To do this exercise, we take actual 2007–2017 annual job growth for each county, and add a fake extra 2 percentage points for the distressed counties. The evaluation challenge is that counties with a higher employment rate might have higher job growth, so distressed counties would have lower job growth without the program.

For RDD, we take some "bandwidth" around the cutoff and estimate how job growth varies with the prior employment rate, both below and above the cutoff. Figure 5.1 shows a bandwidth of plus or minus 16.4 percent around the cutoff of 50.6 percent. The vertical line at 0 represents the cutoff, and the values on the horizontal axis are the employment rates of groups of counties relative to the cutoff.

The two upward sloped lines show that within this bandwidth, job growth from 2007 to 2017 tends to be higher in counties with higher employment rates. The "jump" in job growth is 2.1 percentage points at the cutoff. The standard error of this estimate is 0.8 percentage points, so this estimate is statistically significant. Similar estimates are obtained for other bandwidths.

To illustrate the fit, the figure's points each represent four counties, where counties are grouped by their 2007 employment rate. Each point shows the average 2007 employment rate, and average 2007–

76 Bartik

> **Box 5.3 (continued)**
>
> 2017 annual job growth rate, for a group of four counties. Showing all 83 counties would make the figure noisier.
>
> RDD can detect this hypothetical effect of 2 percent, but the estimate is noisy. The standard error of 0.8 percent suggests that the program effect would have to be 1.6 percent to detect a significant effect with Michigan-only data. In the original data, the range between the 10th and 90th percentile of annual county job growth is from minus 0.9 percent to plus 1.0 percent. A 1.6 or 2.0 percent effect is large relative to this variation.
>
> With data from counties in all 50 states, precision would improve by about the square root of the increased sample size, or about seven times. With national data, standard errors might be one-seventh of the Michigan errors, or 0.1–0.2 percent. We might be able to detect job growth effects of 0.4 percent or less. In practice, what would be detectable would vary with success measures and the time period.

Figure 5.1 "Effects" of Hypothetical Job Growth Program in Michigan Counties, Estimated Using Regression-Discontinuity Design

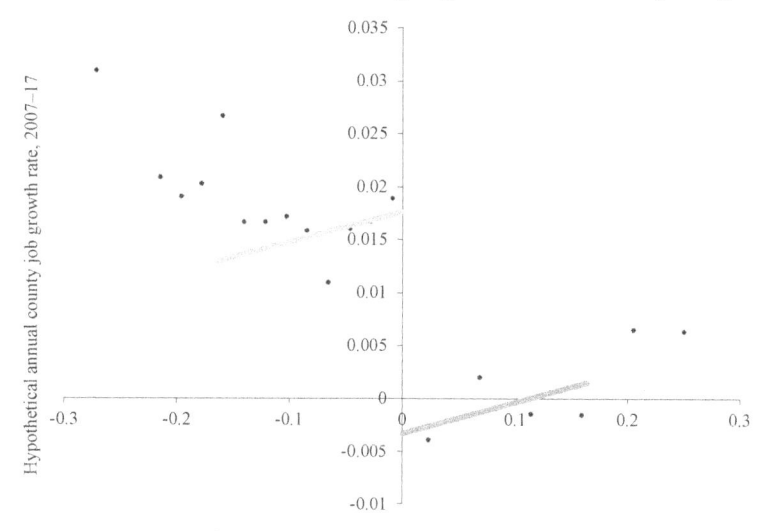

[Scatter plot with x-axis "County employment rate in 2007 relative to cutoff" ranging from -0.3 to 0.3, and y-axis "Hypothetical annual county job growth rate, 2007–17" ranging from -0.01 to 0.035]

SOURCE: Author's calculations.

score cutoff to award tax incentives to individual firms. For incentives to firms, RDD is highly unlikely to be a real option.

For geographic areas, RDD is a more plausible option. Quantitative cutoffs have been used in the past to identify geographic areas' needs, by both the federal government and state governments. Consider for example federal programs such as the Empowerment Zone program of the Clinton administration, or the Opportunity Zone program of the Trump administration, or numerous state enterprise zone programs. All these programs have based development program assistance on the distress statistics of some geographic area.[105] These past precedents suggest that an RDD evaluation plan might be more politically feasible for geographic area programs.

Box 5.4 Questions to See If a Regression-Discontinuity Design Evaluation Is Feasible

- Is there excess demand for the program's budget?
- Is the program able and willing to consistently allocate funds among applicant firms or geographic areas using a quantitative scoring system?
- Are the likely program effects "large" relative to the imprecision that is expected based on the sample size of program applicants and awardees?

SURVEYS

So, if the econometrically sophisticated methods aren't available, or won't yield precise enough estimates, what is the state analyst to do? What about just *asking* firms about job creation effects?

My tribe of economists tends to scoff at just asking people about impacts of a public program. Their cynical assumption is that frequently everyone has a good reason to lie. But let's look at that assumption more closely for the case of incentives.

In the case of tax incentives, or other cash incentives, there are good reasons to suspect that surveys of incented firms may yield very large exaggerations of job creation effects. All firms will welcome getting additional profits by being given tax credits or cash grants. Firms will want such programs to continue, even if the program really has no effect on job creation decisions. Hence, firms have some good reason, from the political interests of the business community, to claim greater job creation effects than are true.

In some cases, a tax incentive or other cash incentive may even have a statutory requirement that the incentive not be provided unless the location or expansion decision would not have occurred but for the incentive. For these programs, a firm that admits that the incentive was not needed is at some legal risk.

Even if the legal risk is slight, the firm may always be at some political risk if its response that the incentive was unneeded is revealed. Politicians and voters may react adversely to a firm that admits to receiving an incentive payment that was unneeded. This increase in political hostility might hurt the firm's prospect of getting permits for future expansions, or certainly getting future incentives.

Having said that, if you can get firms off the record, they will frequently admit that the incentives they receive are unneeded. I was told by several firms, in not-for-attribution interviews, that the state and local incentives they received were irrelevant to their location decision. For example, one firm told me that their main location factor was the availability of a suitable empty factory near a highway. This empty factory near a highway allowed the firm to more quickly open the new plant, and this dominated all other location factors. This firm received an incentive; it had no bearing on the location decision.

The problem is, can a state analyst really get such not-for-attribution admissions for a sufficient number of incented firms? This seems doubtful.

For customized services, surveys of program effects are more likely to give useful information. If the service is worthless, the firm has no strong reason to lie and claim it was useful. Therefore, the service responses about how the program affected sales, or job creation, or other variables, are likely to provide at least a rough indication as to whether the program is providing useful services. This is important information for a state analyst. Is this particular manufacturing extension service, or small business development center, or customized job training regarded by its clients as a quality program?

Surveys have been used to give estimates of the job creation effects of customized business services. One survey in Illinois estimates that manufacturing extension services have a cost per job created of around $20,000.[106] The other survey estimates that customized job training services in Massachusetts have a cost per job created of around $17,000 (see Box 5.5).[107]

Are such survey-based estimates accurate? As already mentioned, natural experiments suggest that such customized services have at least 10 times the effect on firm costs of simply giving the firm the same dollars in cash rather than services. If we plug this estimate into our model of firm decision making, we end up estimating that it takes $46,000 in customized services to create one job.[108] This cost per job estimate is between two and three times the survey estimates for customized services of $20,000 or $17,000 per job created. The natural experiment results can be regarded as more rigorous, whereas the survey results might be biased because some respondents wish to give a positive response to surveys, perhaps because they are grateful for the assistance and wish to return the favor. Therefore, the comparison suggests that survey results might overstate the job creation effects of customized business services by 2- or 3-to-1.

These results are consistent with another study. The federal manufacturing extension program regularly does surveys to estimate job creation effects. Estimates suggest that a little less than one-half of this survey-estimated job creation is reflected in additional job creation in different local labor markets.[109]

These findings suggest how surveys of the effects of customized business services can be used conservatively. Ask businesses in a

> **Box 5.5 Evaluation of the Massachusetts Workforce Training Fund Program**
>
> Begun in 1998, the Workforce Training Fund Program provides businesses with grants to train their workers, with a requirement that businesses match the state grants. The actual training is usually provided by outside providers, such as community colleges. Annual state spending on the program is around $20 million. Grants average around $80,000 per employer and typically train about 100 workers, with a training period averaging 18 months. The average size of assisted employers is around 300 workers. Over three-fifths of grants go to manufacturers.
>
> The evaluation relied on a survey of assisted firms, asking about effects of the program on wages of workers trained, and on new hires or averting layoffs. The grant cost per job created is around $17,000. Half of the job creation is due to new hires, half to averted layoffs.
>
> The evaluation calculates a rate of return for workers trained, due to higher wages alone, of 5 percent, comparing worker wage gains to the cost of the grant. The rate of return to firms' profits is over 16 percent. The study considers effects of the program on both state revenues, and state public service needs, allowing for expected in-migration to fill created jobs. The annual net gain in state revenue minus public spending needs roughly covers the program's costs.
>
> NOTE: See Hollenbeck (2008) for the evaluation described in the text box. Also see the most recent report for this program: Commonwealth Corporation (2018).

well-designed survey about job creation effects. Then divide these estimates by three.

For surveys of the effects of customized services to be most accurate and useful (see Box 5.6), ideally the surveys should be administered shortly after the services were delivered and the expansion or location decisions were made, as well as directed to someone in the firm with knowledge of both decisions. In addition, the survey should be distributed and collected by a party independent of whoever runs

> **Box 5.6 Factors Enhancing the Credibility of Surveys of Incentive Effects**
>
> - Use surveys for customized services, not tax incentives or cash grants.
> - Surveys should be anonymous and administered by an organization other than the one running the program.
> - Administer the survey when the services provided are more likely to be fresh in the minds of the firm's managers.
> - Attempt to have the survey answered by those in the firm who are most familiar with the services provided.
> - Divide survey-estimated job creation effects by three to be conservative.

the program, and there should be some guarantees that responses will remain confidential. We want to reduce the degree to which the respondent will for whatever reason want to be known by the program for giving favorable responses. This could be because the firm might at some future point want to receive additional services.[110]

APPLYING NATIONAL STUDIES TO STATE-SPECIFIC INCENTIVES

An alternative to an analyst coming up with new state-specific estimates for a program is to rely on the consensus of the national literature. Why rely on hard-to-come-by estimates using state-specific data when there is a national literature with some good estimates of how firms respond to costs?

There is a large research literature on how business location decisions respond to taxes. This research literature suggests that for a 20 percent reduction in overall state and local business taxes, on average we would expect a 10 percent increase in business activity.[111]

This translates into such a tax reduction increasing the probability of a business location decision from 90 percent to the observed 100 percent.

State and local business taxes have typically averaged about 5 percent of the value of a business's productive activity, what economists call the business's "value-added." Therefore, if we assume that what matters to location decision is costs, *any* 1 percent reduction in costs as a percentage of business "value-added"—which would be equivalent to reducing a business's state and local taxes by 20 percent—would be expected to increase the probability of a favorable business location decision by 10 percentage points, from 90 percent to 100 percent.

Applying National Estimates to Tax Incentives

How might we use these estimated effects of business tax reductions to estimate the effects of tax incentives? We first assume that incentives are simply treated as a cost reduction, as if they are equivalent to a reduction in taxes. We then must somehow compare the value of incentives versus taxes, which differ in their timing. The research literature estimates the effects of business tax changes that are ongoing. As described in Chapter 2, incentives are front-loaded, particularly in the first year and the first 10 years.

Some research exists on how business executives discount the future in making investment decisions. Such investment decisions would include business location and expansion decisions. This research literature suggests that business executives heavily discount the future in making investment decisions—that is, their decisions focus mostly on the short term. In making investment decisions, business executives report using an annual "real" discount rate of 12 percent.[112] Whatever dollar cost reduction is delivered one year from now is worth 12 percent less in today's dollars, even if there were no inflation between now and one year from now. (If there were inflation of, say, 2 percent, then the discount rate would be 14 percent.) This

12 percent compounds over time. As a result, even without inflation, a dollar 10 years from now is worth only 32 cents today.

Why such large discounting? The person at the firm who is making the location decision probably won't be working at the firm 10 years from now. Stock prices are heavily determined by short-term profits. An executive concerned with the value of his stock options might be inclined to focus on the short term.

Based on this information, here is one way for state analysts to analyze tax incentives. Take the tax incentive package the state provides to a firm—some schedule of tax incentives or grants by year of the project. Use that schedule to calculate the discounted present value of that incentive package, using a 12 percent discount rate. Also calculate the discounted present value of the firm's value of production, its value-added, at a 12 percent discount rate.[113] Divide one by the other to get what average reduction in costs is brought about by the incentives. To get the "but for" for the incentive for that project, multiply that percentage reduction in costs by 10, based on the business tax literature.[114] Box 5.7 provides two more specific examples of how this methodology can be implemented.[115]

Some uncertainty exists in these calculations. Perhaps state and local business taxes have lesser or greater effects than the average effects from the research literature. Perhaps businesses respond less or more to cost reductions from incentives compared to cost reductions from business taxes.[116] Perhaps this particular firm does not discount the future using a 12 percent discount rate. If the analyst wants to admit uncertainty, the estimated effects on job creation could be cut in half if one is pessimistic, or inflated by one-half if one is optimistic.

This methodology has been applied to evaluate a Michigan job creation grant program. This evaluation found that the program had a high benefit-cost ratio under most plausible assumptions (see Box 5.8).

> **Box 5.7 Two Hypothetical Examples of Using the Tax Research to Estimate Incentive Effects**
>
> First, using job figures for the firm receiving incentives, we make assumptions about whether these jobs persist. These examples assume that the original jobs do not shrink or grow over time.
>
> Second, we use data from the U.S. Bureau of Economic Analysis on value-added per worker in the industry, and make assumptions about value-added growth over time. For these examples, I use the average value-added per full-time-equivalent (FTE) worker for "tradable" industries: $194,000/FTE. For simplicity, I assume no growth.
>
> Third, we calculate the present value of value-added over time. We assume the firm uses an annual discount rate of 12 percent. At that discount rate, the present value of value-added is $1.8 million per FTE worker.
>
> Fourth, we calculate the present value of the incentives. I consider two incentives:
>
> 1) An up-front job creation tax credit of $20,000 per FTE.
>
> 2) A 50 percent property tax abatement for 10 years. At average property taxes, this abatement is worth about $2,300 per FTE per year.
>
> The present value of the job creation tax credit is $20,000. Using a 12 percent discount rate, the present value of the abatements is $14,500.
>
> Fifth, we calculate the present value of incentives as a percent of the present value of value-added. The job creation tax credit is about 1.1 percent of the firm's value-added. The property tax abatement is about 0.8 percent of the firm's value-added.
>
> Sixth, we assume how sensitive business location decisions are to lower costs. The research consensus is that 1 percent lower costs increases the probability of tipping that location decision by 10 times as much. Based on these assumptions, the job creation tax credit will tip 11 percent of location decisions. The 10-year property tax abatement will tip 8 percent of location decisions.
>
> NOTE: These calculations use the 31 tradable industries in Bartik (2017a). BEA data is used to calculate value-added/FTE. The database in Bartik (2017a) is used to calculate average business property taxes.

> **Box 5.8 Evaluation of the Michigan Business Development Program**
>
> Begun in 2012, the Michigan Business Development Program (MBDP) has provided $180 million in grants to 239 projects. The grants are an up-front subsidy for job creation averaging $7,500 per job. About 39 percent of incentive dollars have gone to auto firms, and 34 percent to other manufacturing firms.
>
> This evaluation applied a version of the incentive simulation model of Chapter 4 to MBDP. This included estimating a plausible "but for" and multiplier, and estimating economic effects under different methods for financing MBDP.
>
> The evaluation found a benefit-cost ratio for MBDP exceeding 4-to-1 if MBDP is financed by higher taxes. If MBDP is financed by reducing public school spending, MBDP's net benefits are negative.
>
> MBDP's benefit-cost ratio is higher than typical incentives. This higher benefit-cost ratio occurs for three reasons:
>
> 1) MBDP's incentives are modest, which increases their effectiveness per dollar.
> 2) MBDP's incentives are up front, also increasing effectiveness.
> 3) MBDP is targeted at high-multiplier industries.
>
> The evaluation also considered whether MBDP would pass a benefit-cost test if the "but for" effect were significantly less than the research consensus. Because of high multipliers and the incentive design, MBDP would have net benefits even with a smaller "but for."
>
> NOTE: See Bartik et al. (2019) for more details on the example in the text box.

Customized Services

We can also apply national estimates to customized business services. As mentioned above, we can plug customized services into our simulation model, assuming that their job creation effects are 10 times that of tax incentives. This yields a cost per job created of $46,000.

If this estimate is valid, estimating program effects is simple. Determine how much in customized services the program is providing each year, and divide by $46,000 to get a plausible estimate of job creation in incented firms.

This estimate relies on assuming that the state program being analyzed is of comparable quality to the programs being studied in the national estimates. The national studies were looking at exemplary programs. Perhaps this particular state's program is of lower quality. To be conservative, the analyst might want to do some downward adjustment in jobs created. How much? That's hard to say without more knowledge about the quality of the state program. There's only so much one can do without having *some* specific data or other information on the quality of a state program.

WHAT SHOULD AN EVALUATOR DO?

As outlined in this chapter, incentives can be evaluated by multiple methods (see Box 5.9 for summary). How should an evaluator decide which method to use?

If the program hasn't been set up, see whether it is feasible to adopt a randomized control trial or RDD of sufficient precision to detect expected incentive effects. Under the RDD, access to the incentive program by firms or geographic areas would be based on some quantitative scoring system. The program would be evaluated by using RDD estimation techniques to see how firm or geographic area performance compared just below or just above this quantitative score cutoff.

If the program has already been conducted, see if a natural experiment occurred. That is, were there some firms or geographic areas that received program assistance, and other similar firms or geographic areas that did not receive assistance? If the reason that some firms or geographic areas were unassisted would not be expected to

> **Box 5.9 Summary of Evaluation Options for State Incentive Programs**
>
> - Randomized control trial: firms or geographic areas are randomly assigned to receive assistance.
> - Regression-discontinuity design: a quantitative score cutoff is used to assign assistance to firms or geographic areas.
> - Natural experiment: use unassisted firms or geographic areas for comparison, with reason to believe that who was assisted was due to factors with no direct effect on the success of firms or geographic areas.
> - For tax incentives, use national estimates of how business taxes affect location or expansion decisions to infer plausible effects.
> - For customized business services, use surveys to estimate job creation effects and divide by three to get conservative estimates.
> - For customized business services, use national estimates of a cost per job created of $46,000, but consider adjusting downward based on relative quality of this particular state's program.

predict subsequent economic success of the firm or geographic area, then the similar firms or geographic areas can be used as a comparison group to evaluate the incentive program.

If such rigorous evaluation techniques are infeasible, other evaluation methods must be used. A feasible alternative for tax incentives is using national estimates, combined with state-and-program-specific calculations of how much this particular state incentive program reduces business costs, to estimate the "but for."

A feasible alternative for customized business services is to survey these services' users. A conservative usage of surveys would scale down these survey estimates of job creation due to customized services to account for overoptimism. The research evidence suggests that dividing the survey-projected job creation by three might be a reasonably conservative approach.

If no survey evidence is available on a state's customized business services, we might be able to rely on prior research on high-quality business services. If the analyst has some independent information suggesting that the customized business services are of high quality, the program's expenditures could be divided by $46,000 (in 2018 dollars) to determine job creation in assisted firms. These job creation effects should be adjusted downward if the analyst believes that this particular state program might be of lower quality than the national programs studied.

Either for tax incentives or customized services, the estimated effects on incented firms should be inserted into a model of the state economy to estimate incentive benefits vs. costs. This is feasible to do. The above-mentioned studies, of the Michigan Business Development Program and the Massachusetts Workforce Training Fund, provide two examples. Each of these studies used their initial job creation estimates, and economic and fiscal models, to estimate these programs' benefits.

WE ALREADY KNOW SOMETHING ABOUT IDEAL POLICIES

But even without any new evaluation evidence, we already know a lot about incentive benefits and costs, as detailed in prior chapters. Based on this evidence, what is an ideal state incentive policy? The next chapter outlines such an ideal.

Chapter 6
An Ideal State Incentive Program, Taking Account of Economic and Political Realities

Given what we know about incentives, what state incentive program makes sense for governors and legislators?

A state incentive program's design should maximize net economic benefits for state residents' per capita income. But the incentive program's design should also minimize the temptations for state politicians to direct the program to achieve their own political goals, rather than the interests of state residents. Designing an ideal state program requires considering both economics and politics.

PRINCIPLES

For both economic and political reasons, a state's incentive program should be guided by the following principles:

- **Target firms in tradable industries in distressed areas, and firms in high-tech tradable industries in a few high-tech cluster areas.** Incentives should not go to locally oriented firms that compete with other firms in the same state, but rather to firms in tradable industries, which compete in national or international markets. As described in Chapter 4, state residents benefit far more from incentive programs that target distressed areas or high-tech industries in areas that already have a significant high-tech cluster. New jobs in distressed areas, with an ample supply of workers lacking jobs, will be more likely to go to state residents. The expansion of high-tech firms in an area with a significantly above-average high-tech cluster will have higher job multiplier effects that will create more jobs in local suppliers and retailers. As noted previously, such high-tech cluster communities comprise about 60 or so of the roughly 700 local labor markets in the U.S. Do not confuse high-tech aspirations with current realities!

- **Emphasize customized business services more, business tax incentives less.** Customized business services have more job creation effects per dollar than business tax incentives (see Chapters 3 and 4). The political demand for customized business services is more limited, compared to business tax incentives. All businesses will always demand more business tax incentives or other cash, even if the incentives do not alter business's decisions about job creation. Customized business services only benefit a more limited number of mostly smaller businesses that need such services, and are only demanded if the services have some usefulness.

- **Structure incentives to limit the temptation to provide excessive long-term incentives to large corporations.** Upfront incentives have a higher benefit-cost ratio (see Chapter 4). If the state's rule is that the term of incentives must be limited, governors will be less tempted to strike deals that are excessive, as they will have to immediately deal with incentives' budget costs. Mega-deals with large corporations are politically tempting for governors because of the publicity. But incentives for smaller businesses can be at least as effective at actually creating jobs.

- **Finance incentives by higher business taxes, not by cutting public spending that promotes economic development.** Incentive design and budgeting procedure should minimize the risk that incentives reduce spending on programs that promote economic development, such as public schools. Ideally, a state's choice to devote more resources to incentives should be paid for by increasing the state's business tax rate, which exports some of the costs to nonresidents.

AN IDEAL PROGRAM

Based on these principles, what would be an ideal state incentive program?[117] Here are some ideas for a possible state strategy.

- **Target counties**. The proposed state strategy would target state-funded economic development efforts on appropriate counties. These counties would be of two types. First, the state strategy would target economically distressed counties—that is, counties that by some objective measure lack adequate jobs. Second, the state strategy might target a few counties with high-tech clusters—those whose share of jobs in high-tech industries was at least one-third greater than the national average. For the state targeting to be meaningful, less than half of the state's population should be in targeted counties.

- **Start with the basic services supporting economic development**. Before funding incentive programs to help specific businesses, make sure that target counties have the funding they need for adequate services to support economic development. Such supportive services include adequate infrastructure and high-quality programs for skills development.

- **Next, prioritize funding for customized business services**. Targeted counties could be provided with a block grant supporting a wide array of customized business services. The state funding would have to go to firms in tradable industries. In counties eligible only because they have a high-tech cluster, the assisted firms would also have to be high tech. Eligible services would include manufacturing extension services, small business development centers, business incubators, customized job training, and discretionary hiring subsidies for firms that hire into newly created jobs local nonemployed residents referred and placed via local workforce agencies.[118] The block grant should aim at a funding level of customized business services so that all targeted firms that need such services could receive quality services. Such a funding level would be significantly greater than what is currently provided—at a guess, at least three times the current national $3 billion in such funding, or around $10 billion per year.

- **Make tax incentives totally state funded, limited in costs, up front, open to tradable firms of all sizes.**[119] Tax incentives should be nonrefundable—that is, limited to a business's state and local tax burden. For example, incentives could be limited to be no more annually than the sum of the business's income tax liability plus its local business property tax liability. The term of the incentive should be limited, for example, to no more than three years of the business's income taxes and property taxes. But the incentive should either be legally an entitlement for eligible firms in eligible counties, or else administered so that smaller firms as well as larger firms are in practice equally eligible. One hundred percent state-funded incentives, rather than local incentives, would help the target counties more, and limit impact on local public services supporting development.

For example, one can imagine a state-funded tax-incentive program that would include an investment tax credit, and a job creation tax credit for full-time permanent jobs that exceeded both last year's jobs and some base year's jobs.[120] If this tax incentive program was designed so that its magnitude did not exceed three years of the typical income and property tax liability of a tradable-industry firm, such an incentive package would be about $18,000 per full-time-equivalent (FTE) job. The state/local budget cost of such an incentive package would be less than two-thirds of the current typical state and local tax incentive package. Because less than half of the state would be eligible for the incentive package, total national costs of such incentives would probably be less than one-third of current national costs for tax incentives of $47 billion: total tax incentive costs would not exceed $15 billion.

However, the incentive package could only be taken against the firm's actual state and local income and property tax payments over three years, with no carry forwards of unclaimed credits to future tax years, so if the state's existing business tax system had low taxes, the incentive package would be limited by the lack of any incentive refundability or lengthy carry-forwards.[121] The incentive package would also include some clawbacks if the created jobs and investment were not maintained.[122]

Summary

Table 6.1 summarizes this incentive "ideal" vs. current typical incentive practices. Compared to current incentive policies, the ideal incentive package is more geographically targeted, cheaper, and more oriented toward customized business services. Compared to current tax incentives, the ideal tax incentives would be much shorter term and limited by the firm's tax liabilities but would be more broadly available to smaller businesses.

POSSIBLE QUESTIONS, WITH RESPONSES

Here are some critiques of the design of this ideal package, with my response.

Why do incentives at all? Why not just do skills development programs or infrastructure programs, which often have high returns? (See Figure 4.2.) First, incentives that are customized business services often have benefit-cost ratios that are even higher than skills development or infrastructure programs (see Table 4.2). Sec-

Table 6.1 Comparison of Current Incentives vs. "Ideal" Incentives

Current	Ideal
Untargeted	Targeted at distressed counties and high-tech counties
$50 billion annual costs over all states	$25 billion annual costs
94% tax incentives, 6% customized services	60% tax incentives, 40% customized services
One-quarter local property tax abatements	100% state funding
Tax incentive features: often discretionary, up to 20 years, refundable	Tax incentive features: entitlement, limited to 3-year term, nonrefundable (credited against income & property taxes)
Average tax incentive: 1.3% of value-added	Average tax incentive: 1.0% of value-added
Often no budget limit for tax incentives	All incentives part of state business tax budget

SOURCE: Author's calculations.

ond, the job creation from incentives may benefit persons unlikely to benefit from skills development programs. For example, older workers may benefit because of the jobs created by incentives but are less likely to benefit from job training or education programs. Third, incentives create jobs and higher earnings per capita immediately, whereas the economic benefits from skills development programs or new infrastructure are more delayed. High-quality preschool takes decades to have its biggest benefits. A new highway provides some construction jobs now, but the biggest economic benefits for state jobs and earnings are indeed "down the road."

Why not abolish tax incentives, as customized services have much higher benefit-cost ratios? Customized business services have limits in scale, as such services are only useful to certain types of businesses at particular stages in their development. Tax incentives can be more easily scaled up and are more broadly useful to a wider variety of firms. In distressed counties or high-tech counties, business tax incentives can have sufficiently high benefit-cost ratios for state residents, as shown in Chapter 4.

Why not have a fixed budget for tax incentives, rather than a projected budget for tax incentives that are entitlements to eligible firms? Wouldn't a fixed budget give states more control over these tax incentives?[123] A fixed tax incentive budget, if enforced, would imply that a state might refuse tax incentives for large projects in targeted counties toward the end of the fiscal year, if the tax incentive budget was insufficient. Such refusal does not make much economic sense: why forego opportunities for new investment and job creation? Such a refusal is unlikely to be politically sustainable: What governor or mayor would want to be perceived as refusing incentives for a significant new economic development project?

The ideal package does significantly limit tax incentives by limiting their amount to no more than three years of the firm's additional income tax and property tax liability. In addition, the state would seek to each year project the overall net business tax budget, with tax incentives included in the budget. Net business tax receipts, after these incentives, should be no harder to project for state budgeting purposes than is currently the case for business tax receipts. Furthermore, given that incentives will tend to go up with more firm investment and job creation, net business tax receipts should be less volatile with the business cycle than gross business tax receipts.

Why not offer customized business services statewide, as such services appear to have a high benefit-cost ratio even when unemployment is low? Local economic development authorities in nontargeted counties should certainly be permitted to offer customized business services. However, state funding should be restricted to targeted counties, as the benefit-cost ratio for such services is much higher in such counties. In addition, for distressed counties, local economic development authorities will have a harder time financing such services. In nondistressed counties, the local revenue base to pay for such services is more adequate.

Why not make tax incentives discretionary, so that economic developers can better target incentives on firms whose location decisions are more footloose, or whose multipliers or other benefits for the states are higher? In my view, economic developers do not have enough knowledge to know when an incentive is truly needed to tip a location decision. The firm knows its location options; the economic developer is not privy to such knowledge. Economic developers are not mind readers.

Our knowledge about firms' multipliers and effects on local employment-to-population ratios is also limited. As discussed in Chapter 3, commonly used input-output models and econometric models of multipliers and local labor market effects do not reflect many complexities of local economies that may alter economic effects of job growth. Our knowledge about incentive benefits vs. costs is not reliable enough to fine-tune the incentives to each and every firm.

What we do know is that incentives have higher returns if targeted at distressed counties, or at high-tech firms in a few high-tech counties. We should limit ourselves to the most reliable knowledge in incentive design.

Discretion in incentives is likely to lead policymakers astray. Discretion allows incentive magnitude to be unduly influenced by a firm's size, media clout, or political clout.

Rules are a help to economic development policy, not a hindrance. Rules allow incentive targeting and incentive magnitude to be based on some reliable guiding principles, and to not vary because of political pressures. Rules strengthen the negotiating position of states versus firms in the location game. States can tell firms: here are the incentives we have, and our formulas for awarding incentives. We cannot award you more than what is dictated by those rules, but neither will we be treating other firms differently than we treat you.

Why make tax incentive payments up front, in the first three years, with a clawback? Why not just "pay for results" with incentive payments made over time if the initial jobs are maintained, which is what many states claim to do with their current

incentive programs? "Paying for results" means paying incentives for a long time. Long-term incentives don't make economic sense, as explained in Chapter 3. Firms' investment decisions about location and expansion are myopic, focused on profits and costs in the first few years. Therefore, long-term incentives have too low effects on location or expansion decisions per dollar of costs.

Long-term incentives also have bad political effects. Governors and mayors are likely to be more excessive with incentives whose costs will incur when they are no longer in office. Better to remove the temptation by eliminating long-term incentives.

If the concern is about firms receiving significant incentives and then downsizing, this can be dealt with by including clawbacks. With clawbacks, some of the up-front incentives can be recovered if the firm downsizes.

Will the ideal incentive package have enough political rewards to be politically attractive to governors? Will there be enough ribbon cuttings and media coverage of economic development triumphs? Can the geographic targeting be politically sustained? These entitlement tax incentives still will involve some substantial economic development awards for large location decisions. Ribbon cuttings can be scheduled, with impressive numbers for press releases.

If the tax incentive averages about $18,000 per new FTE job, a Foxconn that promises 13,000 jobs can be promised over $200 million in incentives.[124] That's a lot less than the $3 billion that Wisconsin offered, but over $200 million in incentives is certainly enough for a governor to claim credit in a press release.

If the tax incentive averages $18,000 per job created, an Amazon location decision that promises 40,000 jobs can be awarded incentives of $720 million. This is far less than the $3 billion offered by New York, let alone the over $7 billion offered by other states. However, this incentive award is similar to the $773 million that Virginia offered to Amazon.[125] Such an incentive award is certainly enough for a governor to claim credit in the media.

Virginia's offer to Amazon also shows that it is possible to package infrastructure assistance and jobs skills programs in a way that allows a governor to claim credit. Virginia's offer to Amazon combined an almost $800 million cash incentive with $1.1 billion in investments in Virginia job skills and $200 million in infrastructure investments. These related investments included locating a new campus of Virginia Tech in northern Virginia and making improvements to highways and mass transit in northern Virginia. Such improvements may make it more likely that Amazon will hire locally, given that the local skills development pipeline will be better. But such investments might also more generally boost the attractiveness of northern Virginia to other high-tech firms. This Virginia package probably has a much higher benefit-cost ratio than a pure cash incentive. But the more important point is that the state was able to frame this package so that political credit for attracting Amazon was given for providing these investments.[126]

A more challenging issue is geographic targeting: Is it politically viable? It is hard for a state to completely exclude some counties in a state from a state economic development program. One can imagine that it might be more politically acceptable for a state to offer some support for economic development throughout the state, with higher support for economic development in targeted counties. For example, North Carolina follows a system under which the state's counties are divided based on economic distress into three tiers.[127] The amount of economic development awards is higher in the more distressed tiers, and the local government contribution is less. Geographic targeting is challenging, but not politically impossible.

THE STATE PERSPECTIVE VS. THE NATIONAL PERSPECTIVE

In this chapter, the ideal incentive program has been designed from a state perspective, what maximizes state residents' net benefits.

What about the national perspective? Is this incentive competition a zero-sum game, with no net national economic benefits but sizable government costs? What, if anything, should the federal government do about incentives? The next chapter turns to considering these questions.

Chapter 7

The National Interest

What Should the Federal Government Do about State and Local Incentives?

In this book so far, the perspective has been that of an individual state: What incentive policy for a specific state provides the most net benefits for that state's residents?

But we should also consider the national perspective. Does the state and local competition for jobs benefit the United States as a whole? Does it advance economic efficiency, making the national economic pie bigger? Does it make the national economic distribution more progressive, with greater percentage boosts to the incomes of lower-income groups, or does it make the national income distribution more regressive, with greater percentage boosts to the incomes of the rich? Should the federal government seek to regulate state and local incentives? If so, how should this federal regulation be done?

In this chapter, I argue that from an *economic theory* perspective, the case for federal regulation, the case that state and local competition for jobs necessarily always substantially damages the national interest, is weak. If governors and state legislators were the rational actors of economic theory and always sought to advance their state residents' best interests, they would already have adopted the previous chapter's incentive reforms: more modest incentives that were more geographically targeted, with more emphasis on customized business services. Such incentive reforms would advance not just state interests but national interests.

But from a *practical* perspective, the case for federal regulation is strong. Our current incentives don't serve state or national interests. State and local competition for jobs via incentives, as it is actually conducted in the real world, does damage national interests. But given that we have a federal system, that rightly values state and local government, the question for federal policymakers is how to meaningfully regulate state and local incentives while respecting state and local sovereignty.

IS STATE AND LOCAL COMPETITION FOR JOBS A ZERO-SUM GAME?

A common argument is that the state and local competition for jobs is a zero-sum game, with no national benefits, only incentive costs.[128] A new facility such as Foxconn or Amazon will locate *somewhere* in the United States. The big incentive offers from different states do not create more national job creation by Foxconn or Amazon, they only potentially influence the new facility's chosen state. The incentive costs are pure waste, with no national benefit.

This common argument can be extended from new plants or new facilities to incentives to any tradable-industry firm. Suppose an incentive is provided to encourage a new facility to start up or an existing facility to expand. Suppose the alternative possible choice to starting up or expanding would not be to locate in some other state but rather not to start up or expand. Even in this case, the new facility or the expanded facility will hurt job creation in other states. Because this facility is in a tradable industry, it competes in the national market. This facility's start-up or expansion will take sales away from firms in other states. As a result, jobs in other states will decline. Net national jobs might be unaffected. Again, it could be argued that the incentives are pure waste, with no net national job creation.

This common argument overlooks some incentive benefits. Suppose as an extreme that incentives have zero effects: without the incentives, the same location, start-up, expansion, and job retention decisions would have occurred. Then the incentive competition has no real effects on national economic efficiency. What the incentives directly do is transfer income from whomever is paying for the incentives to whomever owns the firms receiving incentives. The immediate effect is to transfer income in a regressive way. Stock ownership is concentrated among wealthier households than are most state and local taxes. A significant portion of incentive costs are likely to be paid for by households in the form of higher household taxes or lower public services. The average household paying such costs will have lower incomes than the average stockholder. So, the immediate effect of the incentive competition on economic efficiency is zero, other than some transfer of wealth from the average household to the rich.

Who eventually benefits from incentives—what public finance economists call the "economic incidence" of incentives—may differ from these initial distributional effects. The state and local incentives increase the profits of firms in tradable industries. Presumably, this leads to more investment in such industries. The increase in investment in such industries may lead to some upward pressure on wages and some downward pressure on prices. Some of the initial boost in profits may be shifted to benefit workers and consumers. How big is this shifting? Public finance economists don't always agree on who bears the burden of taxes on capital or subsidies to capital, and incentives are one form of subsidies to capital. Most applied public finance economists believe that the shifting would be incomplete. That is, a considerable portion of the true incidence of incentives would be to transfer resources to stock owners and other business owners, who tend to be the wealthy.

Suppose instead that incentives do have some effects on economic activity in different locations. Suppose initially that there are similar benefits of more jobs at all locations. Then the incentives will also cause the national economy some efficiency costs. The incentives lead some firms to locate or expand at locations other than would have been chosen. Presumably, these locations had higher production costs or other disadvantages that led to them not being chosen without incentives. As a result, the incentives lead to economic inefficiencies in the location of business production. Overall production costs in the U.S. economy will increase. This will harm the overall U.S.

standard of living. In this case, the incentive competition is to some extent a *negative-sum* game. And the competition will tend to shift wealth toward the already wealthy. Economic efficiency suffers, and the national income distribution becomes more regressive.[129]

But this zero-sum or negative-sum game argument overlooks the potential for incentives to correct for market failures: various failures of the private market to achieve efficiency. Incentives can correct for market failures by providing needed business services or targeting jobs to areas where the jobs will be more socially productive, as we will now discuss.[130]

CUSTOMIZED BUSINESS SERVICES CAN MAKE THE NATIONAL ECONOMIC PIE BIGGER

The zero-sum game argument made so far assumes all incentives are tax incentives or other cash subsidies to firms. But incentives also include customized business services. If such customized business services are high-quality efficient services—their value to assisted businesses exceeds the government's costs of providing the services—then these services help increase overall national economic productivity.

Consider manufacturing extension services. Such extension services provide smaller manufacturers with advice on various topics: adopting new technologies, reorganizing production, improving human resources practices, identifying new markets. If this advice is useful, then the business may deploy its capital and labor resources in more productive ways. If this productivity increase exceeds the costs of providing the advice, then the net economic effect of the extension services is to increase the overall productivity of the national economy. This more productive manufacturing firm may drive other less productive manufacturers in other states out of business, but that is part of the process of "creative destruction" that makes the overall economic pie bigger and improves the U.S. standard of living.

Similar arguments can be made for other customized business services: small business development centers, entrepreneurship training, business incubators, customized job training. For all these services, the assisted firms may improve their productivity. If the value of this productivity increase exceeds the cost of providing the service, economic efficiency is enhanced.

What is the incidence of this increase in the size of the overall U.S. economy? That is hard to say. Some of it may be in increased profits for the assisted businesses. But some of the benefits will be transferred to these firms' workers and customers, and to workers and consumers in general.

TARGETING DISTRESSED AREAS CAN MAKE THE NATIONAL ECONOMIC PIE BIGGER AND HELP THE NONEMPLOYED

The zero-sum game argument also overlooks that the benefits of local job growth may be asymmetrical across locations. As argued in Chapter 3, local job growth has much greater benefits for the nonemployed in locations that initially have high nonemployment rates.

As argued throughout this book, state and local areas should respond to these greater benefits by having higher tax incentives in economically distressed areas. If this occurs, then the incentive competition makes both the national economy more efficient and the income distribution modestly more progressive.

The higher incentives in distressed areas will lead to more of the nonemployed being employed nationally. This enhances the productive capacity of the national economy. Another way to put it is that the economy will be able to accommodate a higher national employment rate without experiencing accelerating inflation due to a lack of workers. The Federal Reserve will be able to accept a higher national employment rate without being forced to intervene to squelch inflation.

Because the expansion of the economy occurs due to increasing employment of the otherwise nonemployed, the expansion will tend to be distributed modestly progressively. As argued in Chapter 4, the persons who get jobs because of new local jobs tend to be in the bottom three-fifths of the income distribution—particularly in the bottom one-fifth. The benefits from incentive policy will not be distributed as progressively as various social welfare policies, such as expanding welfare, food stamps, or Medicaid, but will tend to increase the share of the economic pie of lower- and middle-income groups.[131]

TARGETING HIGH-TECH CLUSTERS CAN MAKE THE NATIONAL ECONOMY MORE PRODUCTIVE BY AUGMENTING AGGLOMERATION ECONOMIES

Targeting more high-tech activity to areas with high-tech clusters can also potentially make the national economy more productive. As mentioned in Chapter 3, there is some evidence that high-tech firms are more productive if located in a high-tech cluster, and that adding more high-tech firms to an existing high-tech cluster further increases the productivity of other firms in the cluster. Productivity might go up because firms steal ideas and workers from each other, and adding more high-tech firms increases such synergies. These productivity effects of adding more high-tech firms to a high-tech cluster may be reflected in greater job multipliers, and may also lead to greater wage increases in the local high-tech cluster.

Ideally, state and local areas should respond to these high-tech spillovers by targeting some incentives on high-tech firms that are locating or expanding in high-tech areas. If this occurs, these incentives will increase the overall productivity of the U.S. high-tech sector. Because of such incentive targeting, high-tech firms would be encouraged to locate or expand in existing high-tech clusters, where their location or expansion will do the most to spill over into increased productivity of other high-tech firms.

REJOINING THE REAL WORLD: ACTUAL INCENTIVE PRACTICE IS UNLIKELY TO HAVE NET NATIONAL BENEFITS

So, incentives can have significant net national benefits, but only if they are high-quality customized business services, or targeted at job growth in distressed areas, or targeted at high-tech growth in high-tech clusters. The net national benefits would be reflected in part in higher job growth, which will yield modestly progressive benefits. If incentives are financed by higher business taxes, as recommended in the book, adverse distributional effects of financing incentives are minimized. If all states adopted the ideal incentive package outlined in the prior chapter, then our current national competition for jobs would make the national economy grow and have modestly progressive distributional effects.

But let's get real. Actual incentive practice bears little resemblance to the ideal (see Chapter 2). Few incentives are customized services. Most incentives are tax incentives that go anywhere in the state, not to distressed areas or high-tech clusters. More distressed states do not more aggressively use incentives, so incentive differentials across states do little to help reallocate jobs to areas where there are more nonemployed persons in need of jobs. States excessively invest in long-term incentives to major corporations, not because this makes more economic sense, but because it makes more political sense: governors get the political benefits now, and pass on incentive costs to the next governor.

The typical nonemployed person in a distressed area is as likely to lose from incentives as gain. Our state incentive competition distributes jobs both toward and away from distressed areas, with little net effect. The average high-tech firm in a high-tech cluster is as likely to lose from incentives as gain. Our state incentive competition sometimes hurts the United States' most productive high-tech clusters, and sometimes helps, with little net effect.

As a result, in practice incentives produce little if any efficiency benefits for the national economy. They redistribute jobs across states and local areas based more on political accidents than on any economic logic.

With incentives yielding little national efficiency benefits, incentives' major economic impact is to redistribute income toward the major corporations that receive the bulk of incentives. These increased profits for major corporations benefit their top executives, as well as their stockholders, who tend to be toward the top of the U.S. income distribution. Because states do not necessarily finance incentives by higher business taxes, a substantial share of incentive costs are paid by households, through both higher taxes and reduced public services. The group paying for incentives tends to have much lower incomes than the executives and stockholders receiving incentive benefits. Our current incentive system is likely to make the U.S. distribution of income more regressive.

A SIMPLE SOLUTION

A simple solution is for the federal government to outlaw current incentive practices. The federal government could impose the ideal incentive system, as outlined in Chapter 6. All discretionary business tax incentives would be made illegal under federal law. The federal government would select target counties or other target areas in which economic development program efforts must be focused. These target counties would include distressed counties and high-tech counties, as determined by federal criteria. They would be eligible for certain time-limited entitlement tax incentives for firms in tradable industries. These counties would also be eligible for block grants for infrastructure, skills development programs, and customized business services. The tax incentives and block grants could be state funded, federally funded, or some combination.

Whether such a solution is constitutional is debatable. Some legal opinions have argued that state and local government assistance to business could be regulated by the federal government under the federal power to regulate interstate commerce.[132] Such state and local business assistance could be deemed an interference with interstate commerce. Subsidizing a state's own businesses disadvantages businesses in other states. The federal government could outlaw such business assistance, or direct that it be used only in designated geographic areas and only when designed in specified ways.

Rather than outlawing current incentives, the federal government could subject incentives to extra taxes.[133] Any gain in business profits from incentives is already implicitly taxed under the federal corporate income tax system. But the federal government could impose a differentially higher tax on the value of either state and local tax incentives or customized business services, or both, unless these incentives and services meet some federal criteria for being acceptable.

The European Union has an incentive regulatory system that restricts the incentives of member countries.[134] If applied in the United States, the EU regulatory system would make many current state and local incentives illegal. Under the EU system, incentives are allowed only in targeted distressed regions. For example, in wealthier EU countries such as France or Germany, the regions eligible for *any* incentives make up only about one-quarter of the overall national population.[135] In eligible regions, incentives are capped: the value of the incentive, as a percent of the dollar amount of the private investment that is incentivized, must be less than some maximum percentage. The cap increases if the region is more distressed.

BALANCING STATE SOVEREIGNTY WITH NATIONAL INTERESTS

The federal government outlawing the current incentive system, and imposing its own system, seems politically unlikely.[136] Such a takeover also is problematic if one believes that state flexibility and experimentation are desirable. A federal takeover would require extensive regulation of the state and local business tax system. The federal government would also be regulating how the states conduct their economic development policy.

If we already knew the one best business tax policy, and one best local development policy, and if we believed that the federal government was wise enough to adopt these best policies, then perhaps a federal takeover would make sense. But we don't necessarily know the one best tax policy or economic development policy. Perhaps the best policy varies from state to state, with different local conditions. And the federal government has limited wisdom and capacity. It already faces many policy challenges, including climate change, health care, antiterrorism, and immigration. Does the federal government have the wisdom and capacity to also micromanage state and local business tax policy and economic development policy?

Perhaps a wiser federal policy would try to restrict intervention to the cases that most clearly affect national interests. And perhaps a more politically acceptable federal intervention would not outlaw or penalize incentives, but rather reward states for better state policy. In other words: carrots not sticks. This would give the states flexibility to ignore the carrots. And federal policymakers would have more political rewards from handing out carrots than using sticks.

The national interest is most clearly at stake for incentives to large corporations. In recent years, large corporations have acquired increased market power. Many markets are less competitive. A few large corporations dominate many markets, with great power to set prices and wages. Recent economic research suggests that this increased market power may have reduced long-term investment in R&D and worker training, increased consumer prices, and reduced worker wages.[137]

Because state and local incentives are disproportionately awarded to large corporations, the market power of such corporations is further strengthened. Amazon or Google or Microsoft or General Motors or

Boeing are far more likely to get large incentives than are smaller firms. Is this in the national interest? Probably not.

Long-term incentives to large corporations pose the greatest temptation for state excess. A governor can attract great media attention and political support with such incentives, yet postpone costs to their successor.

Focusing federal intervention on incentives to the largest corporations is also more manageable for federal regulators. Fewer than 1,500 firms in the United States have more than 10,000 employees nationally.[138] Yet such firms probably get over one-half of all state and local incentives.[139] It is easier to regulate incentives for these relatively few firms than to deal with every case of state and local assistance to individual businesses.

Restrictions on long-term incentives to large corporations could be made a condition of receiving federal grants. This could be a condition incorporated into existing programs, such as the federal community development block grant program, or grants from the U.S. Economic Development Administration, as has been proposed.[140] Or it could be a condition incorporated into a new federal initiative to support economic development in targeted areas, which I will now outline.

As I have argued in this book, there is a national interest in targeting more job growth to distressed areas, and in targeting more high-tech growth to high-tech clusters. A new federal program to target such growth in such areas could make sense. But the devil's in the details, to which we now turn.

A NATIONAL PROPOSAL

Since the 2016 presidential election, national interest has grown in regard to how to help distressed regions. Some cities have been hard hit by manufacturing decline, some regions have been hit by the decline of coal mining, and many rural areas and smaller communities have lost jobs to bigger cities.

A wide variety of proposals have been made for federal initiatives to revitalize distressed areas. These proposals range from funding for infrastructure, public jobs, privately subsidized jobs, manufacturing extension, small business development, high-tech cluster development, and customized job training.[141]

National interest is also great in helping strengthen our existing high-tech clusters. Concerns have been expressed that current housing supply shortages in such clusters (e.g., Silicon Valley) are restricting the growth of these clusters, thereby damaging U.S. productivity and GDP growth.[142]

Distressed areas and high-tech clusters are diverse. Different areas probably have quite different needs. Some areas may most need more infrastructure. Other areas may most need greater housing supply. Still other areas may most need higher-quality customized business services. Some areas may most need enhanced skills development programs.

For the federal government to flexibly address these diverse problems, one possibility is for a federal block grant program to states to help designated counties. States would be required to identify counties that would qualify as being distressed or high-tech clusters. Block grants would go from the federal government to the states to the designated counties. Block grants could be used flexibly for a variety of programs that address local development needs. These programs could include all those mentioned above: infrastructure, housing, customized business services, and job training.

Federal funding and state match requirements could vary with the overall economic distress of the state. States would be required to restrict designated counties so that no more than half of the state's population was eligible for assistance.

As a condition for receiving these federal block grants, states would have to agree to forego providing *discretionary* tax incentives to large corporations (10,000 national employees or more) that exceeded some set size. The size could be set as so many dollars per job. States would continue to be free to have investment tax credits or job creation tax credits that are *entitlements* that go to firms of all sizes, but they would be restricted on any incentive that is discretionary, and which tends by law or practice to differentially go to large firms. Governors and legislators could continue to assist the distressed areas in their state—the Flints or East St. Louis's or troubled rural counties—but not in a way that differentially favors large corporations over smaller businesses. The federal government could enforce this by monitoring incentive awards and deciding whether they in fact are differentially awarded to larger firms. Given the limited number of large corporations involved, such monitoring is feasible.

A meaningful federal program to help these targeted areas probably would have an annual cost of at least $10–$20 billion. This amount is consistent with likely job needs of distressed areas.[143] This amount is also consistent with scaled-up versions of previous federal regional economic development efforts, such as TVA.[144]

For evaluation purposes, states would be required to select distressed counties, or high-tech counties, using a quantitative cutoff. This would allow national evaluators to estimate the program's average effect. As previously discussed, with a quantitative cutoff for program eligibility, an RDD can estimate the program's effect at the cutoff. Intuitively, the quantitative score and the cutoff would be used to predict how county performance on job and wage growth, and other indicators, differ between counties just below or just above the cutoff for eligibility.

By adopting this program (see summary in Box 7.1), the federal government would be encouraging the states to target job growth in counties where it will have greater benefits, either in helping the currently nonemployed get jobs, or in increasing the productivity of U.S. high-tech clusters. And this program would provide a valuable carrot for encouraging states to forego the excessive long-term tax incentives to large corporations. Over time, evaluation evidence would show how these economic development efforts are shaping economic growth.

Box 7.1 Summary of Proposed National Economic Development Program

- **Federal block grant** of between $10 billion and $20 billion annually, to help states assist designated distressed counties, or target a few high-tech counties, with two strings attached.
- **String 1**: For states to receive a block grant, they must agree to forego giving discretionary incentives exceeding some maximum size to large corporations.
- **String 2**: For states to receive a block grant, they must agree to target counties using quantitative criteria, to allow for better program evaluation.

MOVING ON FROM THE IDEAL

This chapter and the previous chapter considered incentive policies that are "ideal" for the federal government and for an individual state government. But how in practice can we get closer to these ideals? The next chapter turns to this question.

Chapter 8
A Practical Path Forward

Many current incentives are wasteful. Excessive long-term incentives to large corporations, which are awarded regardless of industry or location, are not an effective way to increase economic growth. These incentives mainly redistribute money and power to large corporations and their owners.

Current incentive policies have good alternatives. Scaled-back tax incentives can be useful in needy areas or to boost high-tech clusters. High-quality business services to smaller businesses, such as manufacturing extension services and small business development centers, can cost-effectively boost job growth.

But how do we get to these good alternatives? Current incentive policies are politically popular. Voters like their governors and mayors to "do something" to create more jobs. Because current incentive policies are popular and easy to implement—it's not hard to promise lots of cash to a few major corporations for the next 20 years—they are hard to reform. What can move us toward the needed incentive reforms?

TRANSPARENCY

Voters might like incentives less if they knew more about them.[145] Right now, voters might not fully understand incentives' costs, or the failure of many incentives to achieve their job creation goals.

State and local governments should fully disclose all incentive deals. This includes disclosing exactly how much in assistance was promised to the individual firm, how much job creation was promised, and how much in assistance and job creation actually occurred.

Transparency has increased in recent years. Some state websites give detailed reports on individual incentive deals. This disclosure is often mandated by legislative requirements.

In 2015, the Government Accounting Standards Board mandated that to meet generally accepted accounting principles, state and local governments must annually disclose the aggregate annual dollar costs of many incentives.[146] This measure should help transparency. However, disclosure of both the promises and outcomes of *individual* deals is also needed.

Does transparency help the cause of incentive reform? Consider the recent Amazon controversy. Amazon in 2018 tentatively decided to locate two major facilities, one in New York and one in Virginia. Then in 2019, Amazon backed out of the New York decision. It is unclear why, but part of it was that the New York deal seemed to attract political controversy.

Perhaps one reason for the controversy was an accident: due to the simultaneous announcement of the Virginia and New York location decisions, it became clear to the voters of New York that they were paying four times as much in incentives per job as Virginia—$3 billion in tax incentives in New York vs. $800 million in Virginia, for about the same number of jobs. No clear rationale was apparent for why New York should pay four times as much per job. If voters were more fully aware of the costs they are paying for incentives, and how they compare with other states, perhaps there would be some increased voter resistance to incentives in other high-incentive states.

EVALUATION

But transparency doesn't much help if voters are misled into thinking that incentive costs are irrelevant because incentives generate enough tax revenue to more than cover their costs, as is sometimes claimed in current state evaluations. As outlined in this book, we need better evaluation practices, at both the state and local level.

Better evaluations of incentives will point out that many incentives
- do not induce new job creation;
- have only modest multiplier effects;
- generate as much in needed public spending as revenue gains;
- only have a minority of their jobs lead to new job opportunities;
- have opportunity costs for the state economy because of other programs the funds could have been spent on, which might have more effectively boosted the state economy.

States should continue expanding evaluation requirements for state and local incentive programs. Programs should be regularly evaluated on a definite schedule.

The rigor of these evaluations should be increased as much as possible, while being realistic about what is practical in evaluating an ongoing nonexperimental program. States should develop a model of their state economy that enables incentives to be entered into the model, with all their positive and negative feedback effects included. Evaluations should focus on whether incentives increase state residents' per capita incomes. Incentives are mainly a labor market program, which, if successful, boost local labor demand. National research and state-specific data collection and surveys should be used to provide realistic estimates of incentive job creation.

Will evaluation really help promote incentive reform? Some specific evaluations have been documented to lead to incentive reforms. For example, consider the Washington State R&D tax credit. In 2012, the Washington State Legislative Audit and Review Commission sponsored an outside evaluation by two economists, including me.[147] This evaluation found relatively high costs of this credit per job created. The finding led to a recommendation to allow this credit to sunset, which occurred in 2015.[148]

ALTERNATIVES

It's hard to beat something with nothing. If the only obvious way to immediately increase jobs is to offer large tax incentives to major corporations, that's what governors and mayors will do. And that's what voters will demand.

State and local governments should expand and promote alternative economic development policies other than tax incentives. These alternatives include

- infrastructure and land development programs;
- skills development programs;
- customized business services to individual businesses, particularly smaller businesses.

As alternative economic development policies are developed, they need to be regularly evaluated. These evaluations will help modify the programs to ensure they are high quality. The evaluations also will help educate the media and voters and policymakers about what such alternative policies can do to boost state residents' per capita incomes.

In some local communities, it has been possible to develop a constituency for such economic development strategies. Consider Grand Rapids, Michigan, which traditionally has been a manufacturing-intense area, with a manufacturing share of total jobs of about twice the national average.[149] This community's economic development strategy has included the following elements:

- The state of Michigan has made a significantly above-average state investment in customized job training programs for the area's manufacturers.
- Grand Rapids invested in getting a branch office of the manufacturing extension service to locate in the area.
- The area's economic development organization has organized clusters of area manufacturers to discuss common prob-

lems, such as skill needs, and to come up with possible local solutions.

- The local area has Talent 2025, an organization that is encouraging increased investment in local skill development from early childhood through adulthood.
- Local business leaders and political leaders have made significant infrastructure investments in downtown Grand Rapids.
- Local business leaders put up funds to convince the medical school of Michigan State University to locate in Grand Rapids.

The results? There are specific Grand Rapids success stories: for one, a local cluster organization, the West Michigan Medical Device Consortium, helped an auto parts supplier convert to making orthopedic devices.[150] There is overall success in a tough economic environment: despite the problems with U.S. manufacturing overall, the Grand Rapids area has more manufacturing jobs today than in 1990.

A FULL-EMPLOYMENT ECONOMY

Incentives will be hard to reform unless we can significantly reduce the shortage of good jobs. If Americans believe that job opportunities are lacking, there will be a strong push for governors and mayors to do something to create jobs.

When unemployment is low, policymakers and voters are more inclined to "just say no" to costly tax incentives. As of early 2019, there was a new effort to develop an interstate compact in which states would agree to forego company-specific tax incentives. Bills to establish such a compact have been introduced in at least three states.[151] Such efforts have failed in the past, but maybe this time is different.[152] It is probably no accident that such legislation is being introduced at a time when the national unemployment rate is around 4 percent.

THE BABY AND THE BATHWATER

Incentives can be a useful part of an active labor market policy. They can be a cost-effective way to locate more jobs where they are most needed. We need more jobs where the unemployed are located. We need more jobs in productive high-tech clusters. Some incentive designs can promote needed job growth in these places, at a reasonable cost per job.

In reforming incentives, we shouldn't throw out the baby with the bathwater. Communities need a healthy labor market. That requires working on both sides of the labor market. On the labor supply side, we need to make wise investment in better skills development. On the labor demand side, we need to promote growth of more and higher-wage jobs. Our labor demand policies should include smart incentives to individual businesses, both scaled back and geographically targeted tax incentives, and high-quality business services

But there is little danger of incentives being eliminated. A more likely danger is that long-term tax incentives to mega-corporations will be unwisely expanded, to the point where they threaten needed public services, and significantly redistribute income to the wealthy. The baby's in no danger. What's in danger is the house flooding from overflowing bathwater.

To promote broadly shared prosperity, incentives shouldn't be eliminated. But to switch metaphors, incentives should be tamed. This taming requires some cutbacks of what we currently know as incentives. It also requires reforms. Remaining incentives should be more short term and emphasize business services more. The incentive animal needs to go on a more nutritional diet. Only after such taming can incentives make sense. Only then can incentives help build prosperity for all.

Notes

1. LeRoy, Mattera, Tarczynska (2019).
2. There are obviously many ways to distinguish economic development incentives from overall state and local economic policies. But in my view, other definitions are less useful. One could restrict incentives to only discretionary assistance to individual businesses—that is, eliminate any tax breaks that are provided by right to all businesses that meet the tax break's criteria. But in practice, many discretionary incentives are provided almost universally. For example, property tax abatements in Michigan are discretionary, but any significant new manufacturing facility will receive an abatement. Therefore, discretionary incentives are often not much different from an investment tax credit limited to new manufacturing investment. In my view, it is better to include these nondiscretionary incentives if they target particular industries or firms to promote local job growth.

    Alternatively, one could broaden incentives to include corporate income tax cuts that aim to increase a state's job growth. But then, why not include any state or local policy for which some politician argues an economic development benefit? Soon, such an approach classifies all state and local government activities as "economic development." But the incentives that arouse controversy are the ones that target particular firms or industries. This targeting demands a rationale.

    One could include as incentives any policy that favors some industry, not just those that aim at job growth. Maybe a state passes laws that favor some industry because of the industry's political clout. But such selectivity is clearly wrong. What is distinctive about incentives is that they have an economic rationale—jobs offer social benefits—yet are subject to waste and abuse, as targeting "winners" can go awry.
3. As will be discussed in Chapter 3, the latest empirical evidence suggests that many U.S. counties might also be big enough to at least be a distinctive geographic labor submarket.
4. Therefore, I do not consider the recent federal Opportunity Zone program to be an "economic development" program. First, the Opportunity Zone program provides a capital gains tax break that is not targeted at job growth. Second, the Opportunity Zones mostly seem to be no bigger than a neighborhood. Even if the program increases job growth in the zones, it is likely to mostly do so by taking jobs away from other neighborhoods in the same local labor market.
5. Jensen and Malesky (2018).
6. Multipliers will be discussed extensively later in the book. The latest multiplier evidence is discussed in Bartik and Sotherland (2019).

7. This chapter is based largely on an incentives database that I developed. This database is described in Bartik (2017a) and can be downloaded at https://www.upjohn.org/research-highlights/new-database-and-report-reveal-how-much-states-spend-incentives-entice.
8. For more on Mississippi's "Balance Agriculture with Industry," see Freedman (2017).
9. I am not the only policy wonk worrying about this. For example, Richard Florida (2019) raises this concern. On the other hand, the controversies over both Foxconn and Amazon may increase the odds of significant incentive reform, as argued by LeRoy, Mattera, and Tarczynska (2019).
10. The incentives cost data is derived from Bartik (2017a) but updated to 2018 prices. The customized services data is derived in Bartik (2019). Sources include Hollenbeck (2013) and the U.S. federal budget for 2019.
11. Figures on state corporate income tax revenues come from the 2016 Census Annual Survey of State and Local Finances but are adjusted using the CPI to 2018 dollars.
12. This is calculated using the incentives as a percent of value-added figures in Bartik (2017a), using a 12 percent discount rate to get the firm's present value perspective, and then multiplying by the share of wages in value-added for firms in tradable industries in Bartik (2017a, Table 3).
13. Inspired by the folk music duo of Lou and Peter Berryman, authors of the song "Your State's Name Here." https://www.youtube.com/watch?v=EX9p50MIexs (accessed July 30, 2019).
14. Annual tax revenue figures for state and local governments are from the U.S. Census Bureau, Annual Surveys of State and Local Government Finances for 2016, updated to 2018 dollars using the CPI.
15. If every state offered identical 30 percent of wages incentives to every firm, the incentives would not affect location decisions. But in the real world, each state would offer such large incentives only to a few firms, and different firms would be targeted by different states. So, location decisions would change a lot if incentives averaged 30 percent of wages.
16. A more implausible scenario is that business taxes would pay for the incentives. To finance $500 billion in incentives by higher state corporate income taxes would require increasing such taxes over 11-fold.
17. The average percentage that R&D spending is of value-added is 6 percent across these 31 industries. Computer manufacturing is at 23 percent, chemical manufacturing at 21 percent. The only other of the 31 industries whose R&D percentage of value-added is over twice the all-industry average is software and other publishing, at 17 percent. The all-tradable-industry average incentive rate is 1.4 percent of value-added.

Computer manufacturing is at 1.7 percent, chemical manufacturing at 1.4 percent, and software and other publishing is at 1.2 percent.
18. Figures on incentives by firm size are from Chatterji (2018), using data from LeRoy et al. (2015). The distribution of firms by size class is from the 2016 Longitudinal Business Database (U.S. Census Bureau 2018).
19. See Bartik (2017a, Table 10) for state-by-state average incentive figures.
20. In 2015, Indiana's incentives were 2.68 percent of value-added for tradable industries/export-base industries, while Illinois's were 1.35 percent. The employment-to-population ratio (employment rate) for prime-age workers in 2015 was 0.789 in Indiana, 0.785 in Illinois. South Carolina's average incentives were 2.39 percent, versus North Carolina's 0.93 percent. The prime-age employment rate was 0.767 in South Carolina, 0.758 in North Carolina. Incentives data comes from Bartik (2017a). Employment rates are calculated for 2015 from the American Community Survey.
21. Enterprise zones target needy areas, but these programs are small relative to overall incentives (Peters and Fisher 2004). North Carolina has geographic tiers with different incentives, but this is unusual.
22. The incentives model described in this chapter, with results in the next chapter, is described more fully in Bartik (2018a).
23. I am indebted to Mark Robyn for helping to improve this figure.
24. Even if all incentives went to locally owned businesses, such incentives would be difficult to rationalize without local job creation effects. If the incentives had no job creation effects, then the incentive transfers income from the average household to the average local business owner, which would tend to redistribute income upward.
25. Steve Jobs at Apple personally asked Eric Schmidt at Google to stop poaching workers. https://www.theverge.com/2012/1/27/2753701/no-poach-scandal-unredacted-steve-jobs-eric-schmidt-paul-otellini (accessed July 30, 2019).
26. These agglomeration economy effects are a central idea in urban and regional economics (Donahue, Parilla, and McDearman 2018; Duranton and Puga 2004; Kline and Moretti 2013, 2014).
27. Sports stadium subsidies might make sense if major league teams have a significant amenity value to local residents, beyond what they are willing to pay for tickets. If Twin Cities residents just like knowing that the Vikings or Twins are around, then perhaps subsidies for these teams can be justified. But this justification is for the amenity value, not the job creation benefits. See Noll and Zimbalist (1997).
28. If all local businesses in a nontradable industry experience similar local cost increases, most economists would expect the incidence of these

cost increases to fall largely on local consumers, as they are the group least able to adjust away from these cost increases.

What about the loss of local workers' well-being due to higher local prices? Local job growth would be expected to increase local wages faster than local prices. There might be losses for local residents whose incomes are not tied to local prices, for example local residents living on Social Security or pension income.

29. See Bartik (2018d) and Chapter 5 in this book.
30. This could be because the would-have-been incented firm would still make the same decision. Alternatively, a similar number of jobs would have been created by some other firm at the site the incented firm would have occupied.
31. This discussion assumes the incentives go to non–locally owned businesses. If the incentives go to businesses owned by state residents, then the incentives transfer income to these residents. This is a direct benefit to some state residents, and leads to respending by these business owners on local goods and services.
32. More up-front incentives means policymakers will have to decide what to do if the incented firm leaves or downsizes. As I discuss in Chapter 4, one answer is to have clawbacks: provisions in incentive contracts that require some repayment of incentives if jobs are not maintained for some minimum time period.
33. The argument made here is that business executives have a greater focus on the short term than makes sense for policymakers. As discussed in Chapter 4, the evidence suggests that business executives in making investment decisions use an annual discount rate on future real cash flows of 12 percent (Poterba and Summers 1995). The optimal annual discount rate for society to use in evaluating different public policies has often been assumed to be close to 3 percent (see Bartik [2011] for a review). As a consequence, the social costs of incentives, relative to their "but for" effects, can be lowered by making incentives more up front.
34. Specifically, using the model described in Bartik (2018a), the ratio of the "but for" percentage to the incentive costs increases by 38 percent.
35. This statement is based mostly on quasi-experimental studies for manufacturing extension (Jarmin 1999) and customized job training (Holzer et al. 1993). This quasi-experimental evidence is consistent with survey evidence for manufacturing extension from Ehlen (2001), and for customized job training from Hollenbeck (2008). It is also consistent with regression evidence on customized job training versus tax incentives by Hoyt, Jepsen, and Troske (2008). This evidence is reviewed at more length in Bartik (2018b).

36. See Bartik and Sotherland (2019). This study reviews research on multipliers and provides new estimates. It is these new estimates that are used to describe plausible empirical magnitudes in this section.
37. This is true of the many state studies using input-output models. The regional econometrics model of Regional Economics Model Incorporated (REMI) provides multipliers that do include negative feedback effects from costs. However, REMI then adds in estimates of effects of agglomeration economies that roughly offset the negative feedback effects from costs. This is questionable for most non-high-tech industries.
38. This is based on results in Bartik and Sotherland (2019).
39. The statements in this paragraph and the next paragraph about high-tech multipliers, and how they vary with the size of the existing high-tech cluster, are based on Bartik and Sotherland (2019).
40. Using the "Tech 4" definition in Bartik and Sotherland (2019), I would suggest setting the minimum high-tech share somewhere in the 16–16.5 percent of all employment range. The average for all communities (unweighted) is around 12 percent (Bartik and Sotherland, Table 20). The population-weighted average is around 14 percent. As this suggests, the more high-tech communities tend to be larger in population. The 60 or so communities in which high tech is most clustered tend to be larger communities such as the Silicon Valley area, the Detroit area, the Dallas area, the Minneapolis-St. Paul area, and the Denver area.
41. Some researchers have estimated much higher high-tech multipliers; for example, Moretti (2010). For reasons outlined in Bartik and Sotherland (2019), I think these much higher multipliers are overstated.
42. Civic Economics (2007, 2013).
43. An economically booming area is defined as an area at the 90th percentile across local labor markets in the prime-age employment rate, the ratio of employment to population for 25- to 54-year-olds. An economically struggling or depressed area is defined as an area at the 10th percentile.
44. The evidence for these long-run effects is reviewed in Bartik (2015, 2019).
45. Why are in-migrants different from the original state residents? The original residents have ties to the state that cause additional earnings opportunities in their home state to be significantly more valuable than opportunities elsewhere. In contrast, for in-migrants, opportunities in various destination states do not involve different special values for a home state. This argument is made at greater length in Bartik (1991).
46. This job vacancy chain issue is most thoroughly explored in Persky, Felsenstein, and Carlson (2004).

47. How to achieve more inclusive economic development is an active area of research, including the work of the Metropolitan Policy Program at the Brookings Institution. See, for example, Liu (2016).
48. One could also pursue incentives more vigorously when the state is in a recession, and less when a state is in a boom. But recessions and booms end. A policy designed to fit a state's economic situation now may be a poor fit by the time it is implemented. Therefore, it seems wiser to target places with a more persistent lack of jobs.
49. See Burtless (1985).
50. This Minnesota program was called MEED, an acronym that originally stood for Minnesota Emergency Economic Development program, and later for Minnesota Employment and Economic Development Program. For more on MEED, see Bartik (2001).
51. Metropolitan areas are federally designated county groups that are designed to incorporate the vast majority of local commuting flows, and thus to define areas within which almost all effects of a local labor demand shock will occur. However, recent evidence suggests that smaller areas may capture a high proportion of the demand shock effects. Manning and Petrongolo (2017) find that about half of a labor demand shock's effects on unemployment flows occurs within a radius of about 10 miles, and about 90 percent within a radius of about 20 miles. The former would be a little more than 300 square miles, the latter a little under 1,300 square miles. The average county in the U.S. is 2,584 square miles. This suggests that most counties encompass significant proportions of the effects of labor demand shocks within the county, even if many demand shocks are not at the county centroid.
52. Because of the spreading of economic development benefits beyond a neighborhood to the county and then the overall metropolitan area or other local labor market area, we really don't want economic development organizations to be competing at the very localized level, say, among a city versus its suburbs, or between two suburbs. Randall et al. (2018) is a recent attempt to discuss how local governments have tried to achieve broader geographic cooperation.
53. See Bartik (2018a) for more such results.
54. See Bartik (2017b).
55. Legislative Fiscal Bureau (2017).
56. A "but for" of 100 percent is assumed in the models that Wisconsin used to evaluate Foxconn (Baker Tilly 2017; EY Quantitative Economics and Statistics 2017), in the model that New York used to evaluate Amazon (Evangelakis 2018), and in the model that Virginia used to evaluate Amazon (Fuller and Chapman 2018). Some states are beginning to move away from the 100 percent "but for;" for example, Rhode

Island (Goodman and Wakefield 2018; Rhode Island Office of Revenue Analysis 2017), Maryland (Maryland Department of Legislative Services 2016), and Connecticut (Connecticut Department of Economic and Community Development 2014). However, such state analyses are exceptions. Most analyses of state economic development incentives implicitly or explicitly assume that all the incented activity was induced by the incentive.
57. The two quotations in this paragraph are from Kazmierski (2015).
58. Bartik (2018a).
59. All other model assumptions are identical to those in Bartik (2018a).
60. More precisely, the "but for" percentage is based on the research literature that the elasticity of state and local business activity with respect to state and local business taxes is −0.5, similar to the baseline assumption made in Bartik (2018a). This ends up yielding a "but for" percentage of 11.7 percent. This is similar to the 12.7 percent median "but for" percentage found in a review of 30 incentive studies by Bartik (2018b). This overall median is likely positively biased, as many of the 30 studies are positively biased.
61. In addition, the starting unemployment rate is not assumed to converge, contrary to Bartik (2018a). Based on the research by Austin, Glaeser, and Summers (2018), I now think it is proper to interpret the local unemployment rate as being a proxy for whether the state economy is chronically depressed or chronically doing well.
62. Based on the results in Bartik and Sotherland (2019), this appears to be a reasonable assumption for most jobs in most areas of a state's economy. Note that this is the effective multiplier after negative cost feedbacks. The starting input-output multiplier to get this 1.75 effective multiplier is 2.64. This is slightly higher than the 2.50 baseline assumption in Bartik (2018a).
63. The baseline model in Bartik (2018a) found a benefit-cost ratio of 1.22. The differences between the 1.22 and 1.52 figures are due to 1) the lower unemployment rate in this book's baseline; 2) the higher multiplier in this book's baseline; 3) the household tax financing in this book's baseline, versus the mixed financing from various taxes and spending cuts in Bartik (2018a).
64. The model uses a real discount rate of 3 percent annually, which is often used in benefit-cost analysis.
65. For example, in Bartik (1991), the mean long-run business elasticity with respect to taxes (Table 2.3 on page 40) is −0.25, which would be consistent with a "but for" of 6 percent for typical incentives. In Bartik (2018b), the relatively few studies (7 studies) with no obvious bias have a mean "but for" percentage of 6.7 percent, and a median of 3.4 percent.

This lower elasticity is also found in Bartik and Hollenbeck (2012) and Devereux, Griffith, and Simpson (2007).

66. As another example, the baseline model assumes that the project proceeds as planned, and that after 20 years there is some depreciation offset by further incentives. If one instead assumes depreciation of the project from year one—for example, there is some probability of the project closing down each year after year one—then the project benefit-cost ratio dips below 1 if the annual depreciation rate exceeds 2.7 percent. This alternative assumption seems possible.

67. As another example of sensitivity to model details, the baseline model assumes that the elasticity of spending needs with respect to population is 1.0. If this elasticity is 1.17 or higher—public service needs go up at least 17 percent faster than population—then the benefit-cost ratio dips below 1.0.

68. In addition to earnings benefits, property value benefits, and fiscal benefits, Table 4.1 shows costs of about 8 percent of incentive costs due to job growth increasing local costs for local businesses that sell to a national market and cannot pass on those costs.

69. In addition, the business owner losses from higher costs are limited because, first, the model takes a state perspective and therefore looks only at income effects for state residents, so businesses owned out of state are not counted. Second, the model assumes that for businesses that sell to a local market, any higher costs are passed on in higher product prices. As a result, the business owner loss is only for locally owned businesses selling to a national market, which is a distinct minority of overall business ownership.

70. Specifically, the model estimates that 72 percent of the increased earnings is due to increased employment rates, and the other 28 percent is due to increased real wages. The higher percentage for employment rate effects is largely because the evidence suggests that employment rate effects are persistent, whereas the evidence for persistent real wage effects is weaker.

71. My data on baseline income shares come from the U.S. Congressional Budget Office (2016), and my use of CBO data is discussed in Bartik (2018a).

72. The assumptions made to generate distributional effects of changes in different local income types are discussed in Bartik (2018a).

73. See Bartik (1994), which shows that the income and earnings benefits from metropolitan job growth are focused on the bottom three income quintiles, but then drop off as one gets to the highest two income quintiles.

74. This is explicitly shown in Bartik (1994).

75. See Ianchovichina and Lundstrom (2009).
76. See Berube et al. (2019).
77. For example, see the mission statement of the Funders' Network, a group of dozens of leading U.S. foundations that aims at promoting "environmentally sustainable, socially equitable and economically prosperous regions and communities." https://www.fundersnetwork.org/about/mission-strategy/ (accessed July 30, 2019).
78. See https://en.wikipedia.org/wiki/Inclusive_growth (accessed July 30, 2019).
79. This assumes that wages per job are the same for the total jobs created as for the incented jobs.
80. In theory, the 3 percent annual real discount rate adequately takes account of these trade-offs between benefits and costs this year versus benefits and costs two decades hence. However, political leaders may feel they need to attain more immediate benefits than are implied by the perspective of an optimal social planner.
81. See Bartik (2018b) for a discussion of the rate of return to infrastructure programs such as the Tennessee Valley Authority and the Appalachian Regional Commission, as well as a review of other infrastructure programs. Based on Kline and Moretti (2013), the Tennessee Valley Authority created jobs at less than one-twentieth the cost per job of typical business incentives. Based on Paull (2008), brownfield redevelopment can create jobs at less than one-tenth the cost of typical incentive programs. Jaworski and Kitchens (2016) provide evidence that the Appalachian Regional Commission highways boosted annual per capita incomes by 15 percent of highway spending.
82. Bartik (2009).
83. Figure 4.2 calculates ratios of the present value of state earnings benefits to costs for these skills development policies. Only increases in earnings per capita for those staying in the same state are included. The sources for these calculations are given in Bartik (2018b,c). These numbers are further adjusted in two ways. First, I uniformly assume the percentage staying in the original state is 50 percent. The 50 percent figure is conservative. Based on Bartik (2009), this percentage staying is a minimum figure for college graduates staying in the state where they spent their early childhood. Second, the ratios are adjusted by assuming household tax financing and allowing for demand-side effects of both the tax financing and the spending increases. This increases the benefit-cost ratio by 0.07 to account for balanced-budget multiplier effects. Balanced budget multiplier effects are calculated using the simulation model of Bartik (2018a). This adjustment is done so that the skills development benefit-cost ratios are consistent with the household tax

financing assumptions of the average incentive benefit-cost ratio. The skills development benefit-cost ratios are also conservative in that other benefits of these programs, such as fiscal benefits, are ignored.

84. As discussed in Bartik (2018a, pp. 31–32), the research evidence suggests that changes in educational quality have close to similar *dollar* effects on future earnings for different income groups. This naturally gives rise to much larger *percentage* effects for children from lower-income groups. Educational quality may have similar dollar effects because children from lower income backgrounds may be on average more dependent on school inputs for increasing skills. In addition, schools with a higher percentage of low-income children may on average have resources that fall shorter of needs.

85. This analysis assumes that the government should use a lower social discount rate than the private discount rate used by incented firms. The model in Bartik (2018a) assumes that the appropriate social discount rate is 3 percent per year, which is consistent with the research literature. In contrast, the private discount rate used by firms in making investment decisions is assumed to be 12 percent per year (Poterba and Summers 1995).

86. The increase in the benefit-cost ratio, from 1.52 to 2.13, is slightly greater than the 38 percent increase in the cost-effectiveness of incentives (2.13 / 1.52 = 1.40). This occurs because the model has some positive feedbacks. For example, greater employment effects will increase fiscal benefits, which will reduce the negative economic effects of paying for incentives.

87. The benefit-cost ratio increases by more than 10-to-1 because of positive feedback effects in the model.

88. Most of this increase in the benefit-cost ratio is due to the incentive augmenting the profits of local owners. This increase in profits of local owners would probably be skewed to upper-income groups.

89. The simulations of the effects of local unemployment rates on benefit-cost ratios use the model of Bartik (2018a), but with somewhat different assumptions. First, here I assume chronic local unemployment or nonemployment, which I now think is more suited to the problems of depressed areas. Specifically, the simulation assumes the initial local unemployment rate is fixed over time, whereas the model in Bartik (2018a) assumes a convergence to the national average. Second, in the current version of the model, I use the results of Bartik and Sotherland (2019) to adjust the multiplier with local unemployment.

90. Assumptions could be adopted that would increase the effect of local job training policies on the share of the local nonemployed who get available jobs. For example, the simulation reported in the text assumes

that local job training services simply increase the initial share of available jobs that go to the nonemployed by a factor of 1.5. After that initial increase, the depreciation rate per year of the initial employment rate effect occurs similarly to the baseline simulation. In particular, the labor force participation rate effect is assumed to depreciate based on average mortality rates and out-migration rates (Bartik 2018a). Suppose we instead assumed that better training services could prevent any depreciation of the initial labor force participation effect. Then the benefit-cost ratio for incentives would increase to 3.38. But it is not clear that we know how to do this.

91. One could argue that more effective local job training will also increase the local job multiplier. However, I know of no evidence for this.
92. Pew Charitable Trusts (2017) provides examples of state evaluations of incentives, with discussion of how these incentives affected policy decisions.
93. These statements on state practices are based on a January 2019 update by Pew to its mapping of state incentive procedures in its May 2017 report (Pew Charitable Trusts 2017).
94. This downward adjustment of multipliers will clearly be needed for input-output models, which do not allow for the negative effects of higher local costs on growth. The REMI model does allow for such cost feedback effects. However, the REMI model also adds to the multiplier by adding cluster effects. The research in Bartik and Sotherland (2019) estimates such cluster additions to multipliers only for high-tech industries in high-tech areas. A conservative approach would be to also adjust REMI multipliers downward by one-third for non-high-tech industries, or for high-tech industries in non-high-tech areas.
95. In contrast, in the developing country context, there are many randomized control trials of different development programs; for example, evaluations of micro-loan programs (Abdul Latif Jameel Poverty Action Lab [J-PAL] 2018). We are clearly more willing to experiment with people and businesses in developing countries than in the United States.
96. To my knowledge, there are only two randomized control trials (RCT) for U.S. economic development programs. The first is for an entrepreneurship training program for disadvantaged persons. The evaluations of these programs have reached mixed conclusions about effectiveness (Benus et al. 1994; Benus et al. 2009; Fairlie, Karlan, and Zinman 2015). This evaluation relies on our willingness to experiment in the United States with disadvantaged individuals, who are usually not the direct targets for economic development programs.

The second such RCT is for California's film tax credit program, in the 2011 to 2013 period (Taylor 2016). During this period, California allocated only $100 million per year for this program. The program initially operated on a first-come first-served basis. However, by 2011, most applications were submitted on the first day applications were accepted. Given this situation, the state of California decided to award film tax credits via a lottery. This "accidental" RCT allowed the California Legislative Analyst's Office (LAO) to evaluate the program. The LAO concluded that the credit tipped 66 percent of the incented film projects. This is for a mostly up-front incentive that averages 11 percent of the film's production costs. The model parameters used in Bartik (2018a) predicts such an incentive would tip about 72 percent of incented projects.

This second RCT is an accidental RCT, which arose because the program happened to be underfunded. The program has since been tripled in size. It is unclear whether this lottery evaluation will be possible in the future.

97. Jarmin (1999).
98. Holzer et al. (1993).
99. This study is by Bartik and Hollenbeck (2012) and is further described in the text box.
100. This TVA evaluation is in Kline and Moretti (2013).
101. This is found in a recent evaluation of manufacturing extension by Lipscomb et al. (2018).
102. See, for example, Wong et al. (2008), Weiland and Yoshikawa (2013), and Bartik (2013). See Lipsey et al. (2015) for a discussion of methodological issues in applying RDD to preschool.
103. For a recent paper showing this, see Chaplin et al. (2018).
104. See Goldberger (1972) or Schochet (2009).
105. However, none of these programs used a quantitative score cutoff to select eligible areas. Rather, they used some minimum distress standard to create eligible areas, and then federal or state officials used subjective judgment criteria to designate program recipients. Furthermore, for most of these programs, the eligible areas were often relatively small—smaller than a county. Therefore, these programs are not really economic development programs that increase jobs in a local labor market. Rather, they are community development programs that improve amenities in a neighborhood.
106. Ehlen (2001). This study is described more in depth in Bartik (2018b). The $20,000 is in 2018 dollars.
107. Hollenbeck (2008). This study is discussed more in Bartik (2018b). The $17,000 is in 2018 dollars.

108. This assumes that the incentives are all up front and that they have 10 times the effects on firm's location or expansion decisions of a cash incentive. The dollar costs of the incentive are then divided by the induced jobs. Dollar costs are in 2018 dollars.
109. See Bartik (2018b, pp. 90–91). The inference is that 43 percent of the claimed job growth in manufacturing extension actually occurred, based on estimated effects of claimed job growth on actual job growth.
110. There is an older manual by Hatry et al. (1990) at the Urban Institute that outlines some useful guidance on how to survey assisted firms.
111. See Bartik (1991, 1992). This is for studies that control for both public services and fixed area effects. These publications review an older research literature. This estimate is also consistent with a meta-analysis of the research literature by Phillips and Goss (1995). More recent studies are consistent with these findings (Giroud and Rauh, forthcoming; Suarez Serrato and Zidar 2016).
112. Poterba and Summers (1995).
113. The firm's value-added would ordinarily not be reported in state data on incented firms. However, the data will usually report such variables as the firm's job creation or payroll creation. The firm's jobs or payroll can be combined with state-specific ratios for that industry of value-added to jobs, or value-added to payroll, available from the U.S. Bureau of Economic Analysis. The value-added should be calculated over an infinite time horizon and discounted at 12 percent annually to the present. This will require some assumption about how value-added evolves over time. If the incented payments are actual payments, contingent on actual jobs or investment, I would advise assuming that the last observed value-added continues. If the incented payments in the study are promised payments, conditional on job creation or investment, I would assume that the last promised level of business activity continues at the same rate forever. Given the 12 percent discount rate, assumptions about how value-added evolves after 20 years are not very important.
114. Bartik (2018a, Appendix D) develops a more elaborate version of the model. The research literature is reporting tax elasticities. These reflect the long-run change in the logarithm of business activity with respect to the logarithm of costs. The "but for" percentage will then be $1 - (1 - s)^{10}$, where s is the cost reduction in proportional terms. As a result, there are some diminishing returns to scale. A 0.1 percent reduction in costs due to incentives will have a "but for" of 1 percent; a 1 percent reduction in costs due to incentives will have a "but for" of 9.6 percent; 2 percent cost reduction yields 18.3 percent; 10 percent

cost reduction yields 65.1 percent, etc. This formulation bounds the maximum effect at 100 percent.

115. As mentioned before, if we apply this to the average total incentive package in the U.S., which averages 1.2 percent of the value of production over an infinite time horizon, we get the result that the "but for" is about 12 percentage points. This passes a sniff test. It seems likely that a 1.2 percent change in a business's production costs would have some effect but would not in most cases be the decisive factor.
On the other hand, when this approach is applied to cases such as Foxconn, it yields much larger effects. The Foxconn incentives were over 30 percent of the firm's wage bill over 20 years. My estimates suggest that these massive incentives yielded a "but for" of over 70 percentage points—that is, without the incentives, the chances of Wisconsin securing Foxconn would have been less than 30 percent.

116. Businesses might respond more to incentives than to taxes if state economic development staff can be mind readers and target incentives on firms that are more likely to have a good alternative location outside the state. Businesses might respond less to incentives than to taxes if incentives are seen as a more temporary feature of a state's business climate than is the state's business tax system.

117. The ideal state program outlined here is consistent with some other proposals, such as Liu (2016).

118. These discretionary hiring subsidies, with accompanying screening and training services, are modeled after the Minnesota Employment and Economic Development (MEED) program of the 1980s. MEED is further discussed in Chapter 3 and in Bartik (2001).

119. Caps are a recurrent idea in reforming incentives. As discussed later, the European Union caps incentives (LeRoy and Thomas 2019; Sinnaeve 2007). LeRoy, Mattera, and Tarczynska (2019) suggest possible caps of between $5,000 and $35,000 per job.

120. In the average state, an incentive package with these characteristics could combine a 3.6 percent investment tax credit with a job creation tax credit of $9,852 per job. At the national average capital intensity for firms in tradable industries, the investment tax credit would be equivalent to $7,837 per job, so the investment tax credit and job creation tax credit would together add to $17,689, which is the sum of three years of property taxes and state corporate income taxes per job for the average tradable industry firm in the average state, based on the database in Bartik (2017a). These shares of the investment tax credit vs. the job creation tax credit correspond to the typical capital vs. labor shares of tradable industries, so this incentive package would provide roughly equal subsidies for capital and labor.

121. My proposed "ideal" incentive program does not cap incentive costs per firm, as proposed in LeRoy, Mattera, and Tarczynska (2019). If a firm creates a lot of jobs, it is unclear why we would want to provide lesser incentives per job because of a cap. I don't think that large firms should be favored over smaller firms in having higher incentives per job, but I also don't think they should be disfavored.
122. For example, one could have clawbacks for up to 10 years following the credited job creation. If the firm's average jobs fell x percent below the initial increment during the 10-year period, x percent of the initial package could be required to be repaid.
123. I have sometimes argued for a tax incentive budget (Bartik 2005), and a budget cap is mentioned as a possible reform in Pew Charitable Trusts (2015) and in LeRoy, Mattera, and Tarczynska (2019).
124. More precisely, if the Foxconn incentive was actually just $18,000 per job, the promised tax incentive would be $234 million.
125. This is for a planned facility that may eventually have 37,850 jobs, according to the various agreements between Amazon and Virginia. The originally announced New York facility would have up to 40,000 jobs. At 37,850 jobs, an $18,000 per job incentive would total $681 million.
126. As pointed out by Liu (2019), Virginia's offer to Amazon seems preferable to offers from New York or other states.
127. See https://www.nccommerce.com/grants-incentives/county-distress-rankings-tiers (accessed August 26, 2019). The tier system has been subject to criticism, as it may not measure distress adequately. See https://www.ncleg.net/PED/Reports/documents/EDTiers/ED_Tiers_Report.pdf (accessed August 26, 2019).
128. The zero-sum game argument is extensively discussed in Bartik (1991, 2011).
129. This argument overlooks that higher overall national incentives, by raising profits from new job creation, might boost national job creation. But we would expect these national job growth effects to be slight. It is easier for incentives to affect business location decisions than to affect overall national growth. Research suggests that the national job growth effects of a given incentive level, as a percentage of business costs, might be 14 percent of the local job growth effects (Bartik 2011, p. 285). This would make incentives extraordinarily costly as a way to create national jobs.
130. The subsequent sections of this chapter examine market failure arguments for assisting individual businesses. This topic is also explored in Bartik (1990, 2019) and Kline and Moretti (2014).

131. If incentives are financed by households through higher household taxes or lower services, the incentives also transfer some resources from the average household to stockholders. However, if the benefits of the incentives are some multiple of the costs, then the progressive distribution of benefits should more than offset these regressive effects. The regressive effect of incentive financing can be eliminated if incentives are financed, as argued for in earlier chapters, by higher business taxes.
132. See Frickey (1996); Hellerstein (1996); Kramer (1996).
133. Such extra taxes have been proposed by many authors, starting with Burstein and Rolnick (1995). Congressman David Minge proposed 100 percent federal taxes on incentives in a 2000 bill (LeRoy, Mattera, and Tarczynska 2019).
134. Sinnaeve (2007) describes the EU system, and LeRoy and Thomas (2019) update this description. EU incentives are also discussed by Thomas (2000, 2011).
135. See European Commission (2013).
136. When federal court rulings threatened incentives in the 2004 Cuno case in Ohio, federal legislation was introduced to overturn the rulings. https://www.cbpp.org/archiveSite/2-18-05sfp.pdf (accessed August 26, 2019). See LeRoy, Mattera, and Tarczynska (2019). Ultimately, the Supreme Court in 2006 voided the lower federal court decision that limited incentives by denying that state taxpayers had standing to challenge incentives in federal court. https://supreme.justia.com/cases/federal/us/547/332/ (accessed August 26, 2019).
137. See, for example, Azar, Marinescu, and Steinbaum (2017); Benmelech, Bergman, and Kim (2018); De Loecker and Eeckhout (2017); Gutiérrez and Philippon (2017).
138. From the Longitudinal Business Database, U.S. Census Bureau (2018). The actual number of such firms in 2016 was 1,491.
139. This is an informed guess, given that these largest firms, with more than 10,000 employees, comprised 28 percent of business employment, and given that the evidence strongly suggests that the larger the firm, the greater the likelihood of receiving incentives.
140. For example, in LeRoy, Mattera, and Tarczynska (2019).
141. To help distressed regions, proposals have been made for infrastructure (Center for American Progress 2018; Smith 2018); public or nonprofit jobs programs (Center for American Progress 2018; Neumark 2018); subsidized job creation and hiring (Glaeser, Summers, and Austin 2018; Neumark 2018); manufacturing extension (Baron, Kantor, and Whalley 2018; Bartik 2010); high-tech cluster development (Hendrickson, Muro, and Galston 2018); customized job training (Austin, Glaeser,

and Summers 2018; Bartik 2010); small business assistance (Chatterji 2018).
142. Hsieh and Moretti (2019).
143. For example, Bartik (2019) calculates that to bring the bottom quintile of commuting zones to the median CZ employment rate, we would have to relocate about 6 million jobs, and that a plausible cost per job of such a job location change would be $60,000 per job. The total cost is $360 billion. If accomplished over a 20-year period, the annual cost is $18 billion per year.
144. The Tennessee Valley Authority (TVA) was the most intense federal regional economic development program. Its peak annual costs in today's dollars was about $1.5 billion per year. The TVA region has a population of about 9 million. If we assumed that a new regional program had a target population of 10 times as great as TVA, the cost of a program of similar intensity to TVA but for broader eligible areas would be $15 billion per year.
145. Transparency has long been advocated by Greg LeRoy of Good Jobs First (LeRoy 2007).
146. Good Jobs First has played a leading role in advocating for this GASB rule and monitoring its progress. See https://www.goodjobsfirst.org/gasb-statement-no-77 (accessed August 26, 2019).
147. See Bartik and Hollenbeck (2012).
148. See Pew Charitable Trusts (2017, p. 21), http://www.citizentaxpref.wa.gov/documents/meetingmaterials/10-09-12.pdf and http://leg.wa.gov/jlarc/AuditAndStudyReports/Documents/13-1.pdf (accessed August 26, 2019).
149. See Bartik (2018b) and the references therein for much more information on Grand Rapids.
150. Atkins et al. (2011, p. 17).
151. See http://www.governing.com/topics/finance/gov-amazon-multistate-effort-ban-tax-breaks.html (accessed August 26, 2019).
152. See LeRoy, Mattera, and Tarczynska (2019) for more on past efforts.

References

Abdul Latif Jameel Poverty Action Lab (J-PAL). 2018. "Microcredit: Impacts and Limitations." J-PAL Policy Insights. Cambridge, MA: J-PAL. https://doi.org/10.31485/pi.2268.2018 (accessed April 1, 2018).

Atkins, Patricia, Pamela Blumenthal, Leah Curran, Adrienne Edisis, Alec Friedhoff, Lisa Lowry, Travis St. Clair, Howard Wial, and Harold Wolman. 2011. "Responding to Manufacturing Job Loss: What Can Economic Development Policy Do?" Metro Economy Series for the Metropolitan Policy Program at the Brookings Institution. Washington, DC: Brookings Institution.

Austin, Benjamin, Edward Glaeser, and Lawrence H. Summers. 2018. "Saving the Heartland: Place-Based Policies in 21st Century America." *Brookings Papers on Economic Activity*, BPEA Conference Drafts, March 8–9. Washington, DC: Brookings Institution.

Azar, José, Ioana Marinescu, and Marshall I. Steinbaum. 2017. "Labor Market Concentration." NBER Working Paper No. 24147. Cambridge, MA: National Bureau of Economic Research.

Baker Tilly. 2017. *Project Flying Eagle: Updated Limited Scope Report.* Report prepared for Wisconsin Economic Development Corporation. Madison: Wisconsin Economic Development Corporation.

Baron, E. Jason, Shawn Kantor, and Alexander Whalley. 2018. "Extending the Reach of Research Universities: A Proposal for Productivity Growth in Lagging Communities." In *Place-Based Policies for Shared Economic Growth*, Jay Shambaugh and Ryan Nunn, eds. Washington, DC: Brookings Institution, The Hamilton Project, pp. 157–184.

Bartik, Timothy J. 1990. "The Market Failure Approach to Regional Economic Development Policy." *Economic Development Quarterly* 4(4): 361–370.

———. 1991. *Who Benefits from State and Local Economic Development Policies?* Kalamazoo, MI: W.E. Upjohn Institute for Employment Research.

———. 1992. "The Effects of State and Local Taxes on Economic Development: A Review of Recent Research." *Economic Development Quarterly* 6(1): 102–110.

———. 1994. "The Effects of Metropolitan Job Growth on the Size Distribution of Family Income." *Journal of Regional Science* 34(4): 483–501.

———. 2001. *Jobs for the Poor: Can Labor Demand Policies Help?* New York: Russell Sage Foundation.

———. 2005. "Solving the Problems of Economic Development Incentives." *Growth and Change* 36(2): 139–166.

———. 2009. "What Proportion of Children Stay in the Same Location as

Adults, and How Does This Vary across Location and Groups?" Upjohn Institute Working Paper No. 09-145. Kalamazoo, MI: W.E. Upjohn Institute for Employment Research.

———. 2010. "Bringing Jobs to People: How Federal Policy Can Target Job Creation for Economically Distressed Areas." The Hamilton Project Discussion Paper. Washington, DC: Brookings Institution.

———. 2011. *Investing in Kids: Early Childhood Programs and Local Economic Development.* Kalamazoo, MI: W.E. Upjohn Institute for Employment Research.

———. 2013. "Effects of the Pre-K Program of Kalamazoo County Ready 4s on Kindergarten Entry Test Scores: Estimates Based on Data from the Fall of 2011 and the Fall of 2012." Upjohn Institute Working Paper No. 13-198. Kalamazoo, MI: W.E. Upjohn Institute for Employment Research.

———. 2015. "How Effects of Local Labor Demand Shocks Vary with the Initial Local Unemployment Rate." *Growth and Change* 46(4): 529–557.

———. 2017a. "A New Panel Database on Business Incentives for Economic Development Offered by State and Local Governments in the United States." Report prepared for the Pew Charitable Trusts. Philadelphia: Pew Charitable Trusts.

———. 2017b. "New Evidence on State Fiscal Multipliers: Implications for State Policies." Upjohn Institute Working Paper No. 17-275. Kalamazoo, MI: W.E. Upjohn Institute for Employment Research.

———. 2018a. *Who Benefits from Economic Development Incentives? How Incentive Effects on Local Incomes and the Income Distribution Vary with Different Assumptions about Incentive Policy and the Local Economy.* Upjohn Institute Technical Report No. 18-034. Kalamazoo, MI: W.E. Upjohn Institute for Employment Research.

———. 2018b. *What Works to Help Manufacturing-Intensive Local Economies?* Upjohn Institute Technical Report No. 18-035. Kalamazoo, MI: W.E. Upjohn Institute for Employment Research.

———. 2018c. *Helping Manufacturing-Intensive Communities: What Works?* Report prepared for Center on Budget and Policy Priorities, summarizing Technical Report No. 18-035. Kalamazoo, MI: W.E. Upjohn Institute for Employment Research.

———. 2018d. "'But For' Percentages for Economic Development Incentives: What Percentage Estimates Are Plausible Based on the Research Literature?" Upjohn Institute Working Paper No. 18-249. Kalamazoo, MI: W.E. Upjohn Institute for Employment Research.

———. 2019. "Should Place-Based Jobs Policies Be Used to Help Distressed Communities?" Upjohn Institute Working Paper No. 19-308. Kalamazoo, MI: W.E. Upjohn Institute for Employment Research.

Bartik, Timothy J., and Kevin Hollenbeck. 2012. "An Analysis of the Employment Effects of the Washington High Technology Business and

Occupation (B&O) Tax Credit: Technical Report." Upjohn Institute Working Paper No. 12-187. Kalamazoo, MI: W.E. Upjohn Institute for Employment Research.

Bartik, Timothy J., Ken Poole, Ellen Harpel, Jim Robey, Cathy Katona, Jaleel Reed, Brian Pittelko, Nathan Sotherland, Mereb Hagos, Lee Winkler, and Allison Forbes. 2019. *Michigan Business Development Program Effectiveness Study.* Report submitted to the Michigan Economic Development Corporation, January 28. Kalamazoo, MI, and Arlington, VA: W.E. Upjohn Institute for Employment Research and the Center for Regional Economic Competitiveness.

Bartik, Timothy J., and Nathan Sotherland. 2019. "Local Job Multipliers in the United States: Variation with Local Characteristics and with High-Tech Shocks." Upjohn Institute Working Paper No. 19-301. Kalamazoo, MI: W.E. Upjohn Institute for Employment Research.

Benmelech, Efraim, Nittai Bergman, and Hyunseob Kim. 2018. "Strong Employers and Weak Employees: How Does Employer Concentration Affect Wages?" NBER Working Paper No. 24307. Cambridge, MA: National Bureau of Economic Research.

Benus, Jacob M., Terry R. Johnson, Michelle Wood, Neelima Grover, and Theodore Shen. 1994. *Self-Employment Programs: A New Reemployment Strategy (Final Impact Analysis of the Washington and Massachusetts Self-Employment Demonstrations).* Washington, DC: U.S. Department of Labor. http://workforcesecurity.doleta.gov/dmstree/op/op95/op_04-95.pdf (accessed August 28, 2019).

Benus, Jacob, Theodore Shen, Sisi Zhang, Marc Chan, and Benjamin Hansen. 2009. *Growing America through Entrepreneurship: Final Evaluation of Project GATE.* Washington, DC: U.S. Department of Labor.

Berube, Alan, Isha Shah, Alec Friedhoff, and Chad Shearer. 2019. "Metro Monitor 2019: Inclusion Remains Elusive amid Widespread Metro Growth and Rising Prosperity." Washington, DC: Metropolitan Policy Program, Brookings Institution.

Burstein, Melvin L., and Arthur J. Rolnick. 1995. "Congress Should End the Economic War among the States." *The Region: Federal Reserve Bank of Minneapolis 1994 Annual Report* 9(1): 2–20.

Burtless, Gary. 1985. "Are Targeted Wage Subsidies Harmful? Evidence from a Wage Voucher Experiment." *ILR Review* 39(1): 105–114.

Center for American Progress. 2018. *Blueprint for the 21st Century: A Plan for Better Jobs and Stronger Communities.* Washington, DC: Center for American Progress.

Chaplin, Duncan D., Thomas D. Cook, Jelena Zurovac, Jared S. Coopersmith, Mariel M. Finucane, Lauren N. Vollmer, and Rebecca E. Morris. 2018. "The Internal and External Validity of the Regression Discontinuity

Design: A Meta-Analysis of 15 Within-Study Comparisons." *Journal of Policy Analysis and Management* 37(2): 403–429.

Chatterji, Aaron K. 2018. "The Main Street Fund: Investing in an Entrepreneurial Economy." The Hamilton Project Policy Proposal No. 2018-09. Washington, DC: Brookings Institution, The Hamilton Project.

Civic Economics. 2007. *The San Francisco Retail Diversity Study*. Chicago: Civic Economics. ilsr.org/wp-content/uploads/2011/12/SFRDS-May07-2.pdf (accessed July 31, 2017).

———. 2013. *Independent BC: Small Business and the British Columbia Economy.* Report prepared for the Canadian Union of Public Employees–British Columbia. Chicago: Civic Economics.

Commonwealth Corporation. 2018. *Workforce Training Fund: FY18 Annual Report and Performance Report.* Boston: Commonwealth Corporation, Massachusetts Executive Office of Labor and Workforce Development.

Congressional Budget Office (CBO). 2016. *The Distribution of Household Income and Federal Taxes, 2013*. Washington, DC: Congressional Budget Office.

Connecticut Department of Economic and Community Development. 2014. *An Assessment of Connecticut's Tax Credit and Abatement Programs.* Hartford: Connecticut Department of Economic and Community Development.

De Loecker, Jan, and Jan Eeckhout. 2017. "The Rise of Market Power and the Macroeconomic Implications." NBER Working Paper No. 23687. Cambridge, MA: National Bureau of Economic Research.

Devereux, Michael P., Rachel Griffith, and Helen Simpson. 2007. "Firm Location Decisions, Regional Grants and Agglomeration Externalities." *Journal of Public Economics* 91(3–4): 413–435.

Donahue, Ryan, Joseph Parilla, and Brad McDearman. 2018. "Rethinking Cluster Initiatives." Washington, DC: Metropolitan Policy Program, Brookings Institution.

Duranton, Gilles, and Diego Puga. 2004. "Micro-Foundations of Urban Agglomeration Economies." In *Handbook of Regional and Urban Economics*, vol. 4, J.V. Henderson and J.F. Thisse, eds. Amsterdam: Elsevier, pp. 2063–2117.

Ehlen, Mark. 2001. "The Economic Impact of Manufacturing Extension Centers." *Economic Development Quarterly* 15(1): 36–44.

European Commission. 2013. *Guidelines on Regional State Aid for 2014–2020.* https://eur-lex.europa.eu/LexUriServ/LexUriServ.do?uri=OJ:C:2013:209:0001:0045:EN:PDF (accessed August 28, 2019).

Evangelakis, Peter. 2018. *Economic Impact of Establishing HQ2 in New York State.* Report to Empire State Development. Amherst, MA, and Washington, DC: Regional Economic Models, Inc.

EY Quantitative Economics and Statistics. 2017. *Quantifying Project Flying Eagle's Potential Economic Impacts in Wisconsin.* Confidential report.

Fairlie, Robert W., Dean Karlan, and Jonathan Zinman. 2015. "Behind the GATE Experiment: Evidence on Effects of and Rationales for Subsidized Entrepreneurship Training." *American Economic Journal: Economic Policy 2015* 7(2): 125–161.

Florida, Richard. 2019. "6 Rules for Better, More Inclusive Economic Development in Cities." CityLab, February 26. https://www.citylab.com/perspective/2019/02/amazon-hq2-new-york-incentives-economic-development-cities/583540/ (accessed August 28, 2019).

Freedman, Matthew. 2017. "Persistence in Industrial Policy Impacts: Evidence from Depression-Era Mississippi." *Journal of Urban Economics* 102(C): 34–51.

Frickey, Phillip. 1996. "The Congressional Process and the Constitutionality of Federal Legislation to End the Economic War among the States." *The Region.* Minneapolis: Federal Reserve Bank of Minneapolis.

Fuller, Stephen, and Jeannette Chapman. 2018. *The Economic and Fiscal Impacts of Locating Amazon's HQ2 in Arlington County, Virginia.* Arlington, VA: Report to the Virginia Economic Development Partnership, Stephen S. Fuller Institute and the Schar School of Policy and Government, George Mason University.

Giroud, Xavier, and Joshua Rauh. Forthcoming. "State Taxation and the Reallocation of Business Activity: Evidence from Establishment-Level Data." *Journal of Political Economy.*

Glaeser, Edward L., Lawrence H. Summers, and Ben Austin. 2018. "A Rescue Plan for a Jobs Crisis in the Heartland." *New York Times*, May 24. https://www.nytimes.com/2018/05/24/opinion/heartland-wage-subsidy-rust-belt.html (accessed August 1, 2019).

Goldberger, A.S. 1972. "Selection Bias in Evaluating Treatment Effects: Some Formal Illustrations." Discussion Paper No. 129–172. Madison: University of Wisconsin–Madison, Institute for Research on Poverty.

Goodman, Josh, and Alison Wakefield. 2018. "Rhode Island Tax Incentive Evaluations Give Lawmakers Valuable Insights." Philadelphia: Pew Charitable Trusts. https://www.pewtrusts.org/en/research-and-analysis/articles/2018/10/01/rhode-island-tax-incentive-evaluations-give-lawmakers-valuable-insights (accessed September 12, 2019).

Gutiérrez, Germán, and Thomas Philippon. 2017. "Investment-Less Growth: An Empirical Investigation." NBER Working Paper No. 22897. Cambridge, MA: National Bureau of Economic Research.

Hatry, Harry, Mark Fall, Thomas Singer, and Blaine Liner. 1990. "Monitoring the Outcomes of Economic Development Programs." Washington, DC: Urban Institute.

Hellerstein, Walter. 1996. "Commerce Clause Restraints on State Tax Incentives." *The Region*. Minneapolis: Federal Reserve Bank of Minneapolis.

Hendrickson, Clara, Mark Muro, and William A. Galston. 2018. *Countering the Geography of Discontent: Strategies for Left-Behind Places*. Washington, DC: Brookings Institution.

Hollenbeck, Kevin. 2008. "Is There a Role for Public Support of Incumbent Worker On-the-Job Training?" Upjohn Institute Working Paper No. 08-138. Kalamazoo, MI: W.E. Upjohn Institute for Employment Research.

———. 2013. "Public Support of Workforce Training for Incumbent Workers? Paper. College Park: School of Public Policy, University of Maryland.

Holzer, Harry J., Richard N. Block, Marcus Cheatham, and Jack H. Knott. 1993. "Are Training Subsidies for Firms Effective? The Michigan Experience." *Industrial and Labor Relations Review* 46(4): 625–636.

Hoyt, William H., Christopher Jepsen, and Kenneth R. Troske. 2008. "Business Incentives and Employment: What Incentives Work and Where?" IFIR Working Paper No. 2009-02. Lexington: University of Kentucky, James W. Martin School of Public Policy and Administration, Institute for Federalism and Intergovernmental Relations.

Hsieh, Chang-Tai, and Enrico Moretti. 2019. "Housing Constraints and Spatial Misallocation." *American Economic Journal: Macroeconomics* 11(2): 1–39.

Ianchovichina, Elena, and Susanna Lundstrom. 2009. "What Is Inclusive Growth?" Memorandum. Washington, DC: World Bank. http://siteresources.worldbank.org/intdebtdept/Resources/468980-1218567884549/WhatIsInclusiveGrowth20081230.pdf (accessed September 8, 2019).

Jarmin, Ronald S. 1999. "Evaluating the Impact of Manufacturing Extension on Productivity Growth." *Journal of Policy Analysis and Management* 18(1): 99–119.

Jaworski, Taylor, and Carl T. Kitchens. 2016. "National Policy for Regional Development: Evidence from Appalachian Highways." NBER Working Paper No. 22073. Cambridge, MA: National Bureau of Economic Research.

Jensen, Nathan M., and Edward J. Malesky. 2018. *Incentives to Pander: How Politicians Use Corporate Welfare for Political Gain*. Cambridge: Cambridge University Press.

Kazmierski, Mike. 2015. "In Defense of Economic Incentives." *Reno Gazette Journal*, November 12. https://www.rgj.com/story/opinion/columnists/2015/11/12/kazmierski-defense-economic-incentives/75676170/ (accessed September 8, 2019).

Kline, Patrick, and Enrico Moretti. 2013. "Local Economic Development, Agglomeration Economies, and the Big Push: 100 Years of Evidence from the Tennessee Valley Authority." *Quarterly Journal of Economics* 129(1): 275–331.

———. 2014. "People, Places, and Public Policy: Some Simple Welfare Economics of Local Economic Development Programs." *Annual Review of Economics* 6: 629–662.

Kramer, Larry. 1996. "The Power of Congress to Regulate Interstate Economic Competition." *The Region.* Minneapolis: Federal Reserve Bank of Minneapolis.

Legislative Fiscal Bureau. 2017. Memo on Foxconn, August 8. Madison, WI: Legislative Fiscal Bureau.

LeRoy, Greg. 2007. "Nine Concrete Ways to Curtail the Economic War among the States." In *Reining in the Competition for Capital*, Ann Markusen, ed. Kalamazoo, MI: W.E. Upjohn Institute for Employment Research, pp. 183–198.

LeRoy, Greg, Carolyn Fryberger, Kasia Tarczynksa, Thomas Cafcas, Elizabeth Bird, and Philip Mattera. 2015. "Shortchanging Small Business: How Big Businesses Dominate State Economic Development Incentives." Washington, DC: Good Jobs First.

LeRoy, Greg, with Phillip Mattera and Kasia Tarczynska. 2019. *Ending the Economic War among the States: A Strategic Proposal.* Washington, DC: Good Jobs First.

LeRoy, Greg, and Kenneth Thomas. 2019. "Lessons for the U.S.: How the EU Controls Bidding Wars for Jobs and Investment." *Shelterforce*, June 17. https://shelterforce.org/2019/06/17/lessons-for-the-u-s-how-the-eu-controls-bidding-wars-for-jobs-and-investment/ (accessed August 28, 2019).

Lipscomb, Clifford A., Jan Youtie, Philip Shapira, Sanjay Arora, and Andy Krause. 2018. "Evaluating the Impact of Manufacturing Extension Services on Establishment Performance." *Economic Development Quarterly* 32(1): 29–43.

Lipsey, Mark W., Christina Weiland, Hirokazu Yoshikawa, Sandra Jo Wilson, and Kerry G. Hofer. 2015. "The Prekindergarten Age-Cutoff Regression-Discontinuity Design: Methodological Issues and Implications for Application." *Educational Evaluation and Policy Analysis* 37(3): 296–313.

Liu, Amy. 2016. *Remaking Economic Development: The Markets and Civics of Continuous Growth and Prosperity.* Washington, DC: Brookings Institution.

———. 2019. "A Better Way to Attract Amazon's Jobs: Virginia Can Teach New York a Few Things about How to Make a Deal That Actually Works." Op-ed, *New York Times*, Feb. 16. https://www.nytimes.com/2019/02/16/opinion/amazon-new-york.html (accessed August 27, 2019).

Manning, Alan, and Barbara Petrongolo. 2017. "How Local Are Labor Markets? Evidence from a Spatial Job Search Model." *American Economic Review* 107(10): 2877–2907.

Maryland Department of Legislative Services. 2016. *Draft Evaluation of the Job Creation Tax Credit.* Annapolis: Maryland Department of Legislative Services.

Moretti, Enrico. 2010. "Local Multipliers." *American Economic Review: Papers & Proceedings* 100(May): 1–7.

Neumark, David. 2018. "Rebuilding Communities Job Subsidies." In *Place-Based Policies for Shared Economic Growth*, Jay Shambaugh and Ryan Nunn, eds. Washington, DC: Brookings Institution, The Hamilton Project, pp. 71–121.

Noll, Roger G., and Andrew Zimbalist, eds. 1997. *Sports, Jobs, and Taxes: The Economic Impact of Sports Teams and Stadiums.* Washington, DC: Brookings Institution Press.

Paull, Evans. 2008. "The Environmental and Economic Impacts of Brownfields Redevelopment." Working draft for distribution. Washington, DC: Northeast Midwest Institute.

Persky, Joseph, Daniel Felsenstein, and Virginia Carlson. 2004. *Does "Trickle Down" Work? Economic Development and Job Chains in Local Labor Markets.* Kalamazoo, MI: W.E. Upjohn Institute for Employment Research.

Peters, Alan H., and Peter S. Fisher. 2004. "The Failures of Economic Development Incentives." *Journal of the American Planning Association* 70(1): 27–37.

Pew Charitable Trusts. 2015. *Reducing Budget Risks: Using Data and Design to Make State Tax Incentives More Predictable.* Philadelphia and Washington: Pew Charitable Trusts.

———. 2017. *How States Are Improving Tax Incentives for Jobs and Growth: A National Assessment of Evaluation Practices.* Philadelphia and Washington: Pew Charitable Trusts.

Phillips, Joseph M., and Ernest P. Goss. 1995. "The Effect of State and Local Taxes on Economic Development: A Meta-Analysis." *Southern Economic Journal* 62(2): 320–333.

Poterba, James M., and Lawrence H. Summers. 1995. "A CEO Survey of U.S. Companies' Time Horizons and Hurdle Rates." *MIT Sloan Management Review* 37(1): 43.

Randall, Megan, Kim Rueben, Brett Theodos, and Aravind Boddupalli. 2018. *Partners or Pirates: Collaboration and Competition in Local Economic Development.* Washington, DC: Urban Institute.

Rhode Island Office of Revenue Analysis. 2017. *Unified Economic Development Report.* Report for Fiscal Year 2014, State of Rhode Island. Providence: Rhode Island Office of Revenue Analysis.

Schochet, P. Z. 2009. "Statistical Power for Regression Discontinuity Designs in Education Evaluations." *Journal of Educational and Behavioral Statistics* 34(2): 238–266.

Sinnaeve, Adinda. 2007. "How the EU Manages Subsidy Competition." In *Reining in the Competition for Capital*. Ann Markusen, ed. Kalamazoo, MI: W.E. Upjohn Institute for Employment Research, pp. 87–102.

Smith, Stephen C. 2018. "Development Economics Meets the Challenges of Lagging U.S. Areas; Applications to Education, Health and Nutrition, Behavior, and Infrastructure." In *Place-Based Policies for Shared Economic Growth*, Jay Shambaugh and Ryan Nunn, eds. Washington, DC: Brookings Institution, The Hamilton Project, pp. 185–242.

Suárez Serrato, Juan Carlos, and Owen Zidar. 2016. "Who Benefits from State Corporate Tax Cuts? A Local Labor Markets Approach with Heterogeneous Firms." *American Economic Review* 106(9): 2582–2624.

Taylor, Mac. 2016. *California's First Film Tax Credit Program*. Sacramento: Legislative Analyst's Office.

Thomas, Kenneth P. 2000. *Competing for Capital: Europe and North America in a Global Era*. Washington, DC: Georgetown University Press.

———. 2011. *Investment Incentives and the Global Competition for Capital*, New York: Palgrave Macmillan.

U.S. Census Bureau. 2018. *Business Dynamics Database: Firm Characteristics by Initial Firm Size, 2016*. Washington, DC: Census Bureau. https://www.census.gov/ces/dataproducts/bds/data_firm2016.html (accessed August 28, 2019).

Weiland, Christina, and Hirokazu Yoshikawa. 2013. "Impacts of a Prekindergarten Program on Children's Mathematics, Language, Literacy, Executive Function, and Emotional Skills." *Child Development* 84(6): 2112–2130.

Wong, Vivian C., Thomas D. Cook, W. Steven Barnett, and Wanghee Jung. 2008. "An Effectiveness-Based Evaluation of Five State Pre-Kindergarten Programs." *Journal of Policy Analysis and Management* 27(1): 122–154.

Author

Timothy J. Bartik is a senior economist at the Upjohn Institute. His research focuses on state and local economic development and local labor markets. Bartik's 1991 book, *Who Benefits from State and Local Economic Development Policies?*, is widely cited as an important and influential review of the evidence on how local policies affect economic development. His most recent research includes a 2017 report outlining a new database on business incentives offered by state and local governments, a 2018 report on the benefits and costs of incentives, another 2018 report on how to help manufacturing-intensive communities, and a 2019 paper on how place-based policies can promote overall economic growth. Bartik is coeditor of the academic journal *Economic Development Quarterly*, which focuses on state and local economic development issues. He received his BA from Yale University and his PhD in economics from the University of Wisconsin–Madison. Prior to joining the Upjohn Institute in 1989, he was an assistant professor of economics at Vanderbilt University.

Index

Note: The italic letters *b, f, n,* and *t* following a page number indicate a box, figure, note, or table, respectively, on that page. Double letters refer to more than one such item on that page.

Amazon (firm)
  business incentives offered to, 1, 9, 97–98, 122*n*9, 135*nn*125–126
  effect of transparency on, location deal, 116
  evaluation of, deal with "but for" percentage by New York and Virginia, 36–37, 126–127*n*56
  U.S. location potential for, 102, 135*n*128
Appalachian Regional Commission (ARC), as federal infrastructure investment, 48–49, 129*n*81
Apple (firm), poaching workers from, 20, 123*n*25
ARC. *See* Appalachian Regional Commission

Balance Agriculture with Industry program, 7, 122*n*8
Benefit-cost ratios
  alternative incentive policies and, 54–58, 55*t*, 93–94, 130*nn*86–89
  analysis of, in job growth promotion, 36, 135*n*129
  better, with infrastructure and skills development programs, 48–51, 50*f*, 80*b*, 129–130*n*83
  business incentive model with, 40–41, 127–128*n*65, 127*nn*63–64, 128*nn*66–67
  higher, with customized services and up-front incentives, 94–95, 94*t*
  reforming incentives to increase, 46–47, 92, 134*n*119
Berryman, Lou and Peter, song, 11–12, 122*n*13
Brookings Institution, 30, 45, 126*n*47, 129*n*76
Business decisions, 25
  "but for" percentage in, 22, 23*f*, 26–27, 36–37, 40, 41, 46, 83, 85*b*, 124*nn*29–35, 126–127*n*56, 127–128*n*65, 127*n*60, 133–134*n*114, 134*n*115
  firm location or expansion as, and incentives, 6, 11–12, 18–20, 19*f*, 37, 81–82, 96, 97–98, 102, 122*n*13, 122*n*15, 127*n*57, 135*n*125
Business incentives
  cost of, 8–10, 9*t*, 34, 116, 122*n*10
  database developed to study, 7, 122*n*7
  firms with tradable goods or services targeted for, 12–13
  fiscal benefits of, 5–6, 17, 21–22, 33–34, 41, 42*t*, 128*n*68
  long-term *vs.* up-front, and policy, 14–15, 15*f*, 47, 54–55, 55*t*, 90, 96–97, 111, 129*n*80
  needy (jobless) areas and, compared by state, 13–14, 123*n*19
  paying for costs of, 34–35, 126*nn*53–55
  reasons for, 3, 4–5, 50*f*, 55*t*, 93–94, 115, 121*n*2
  reform needed for, 14–15, 46–47, 59, 93, 94*t*, 101, 115, 120, 123*n*21
  (*see also* Business incentives, practical reform of)
  size of, 10–12, 110–111, 122*nn*11–16
  targeted, aka picking winners, 2, 14, 67, 70–73, 89–90
  types of, 1, 8–10, 104–105
Business incentives, baseline model for, 39–45
  assumptions of, 39–40, 127*nn*58–62
  benefit-cost ratio of, 40–41, 127–128*n*65, 127*nn*63–64, 128*nn*66–67
  benefit distribution across income groups, 43–45, 43*f*, 128*nn*70–74, 129*nn*75–78

Business incentives, baseline model for, *cont.*
  benefit distribution across income types, 41–43, 42*t*, 128*nn*68–69
  incentive benefits average close to costs, 45–47, 129*n*79
Business incentives, better policies, 54–59
  effects on incented firms, 54–56, 55*t*, 130*nn*85–87
  financing with fewer in-state burdens, 57–58
  multiplier usage, 56, 130*n*88
  share of new jobs in-state, 56–57, 130–131*nn*90–91, 130*n*89
  synergistic effects of, 58–59
  See also under Public policy, effects of, on business incentives
Business incentives, better policies for average, 47–54, 129*n*80
  high-quality public programs *vs.* average incentives, 53–54
  infrastructure, 48–49, 129*n*81
  opportunity costs of financing incentives, 51–53, 117, 130*n*84
  skills development, 49–51, 50*f*, 129–130*n*83, 129*n*82
Business incentives, ideal state programs, 6, 39, 88–99, 94*t*, 134*n*117
  basic and customized services, 90, 91–92, 94*t*
  critique of, with questions and responses, 93–98, 94*t*, 135*nn*123–127
  financing by higher business taxes, 90–91, 92
  guiding principles, 89–91
  ideas for state achievement of, 91–93, 114, 134*nn*118–120, 135*nn*121–122
  long-term incentives and limits, 90, 92, 96–97, 111, 134*n*119, 136*n*140
  state *vs.* national perspectives on, 98–99, 108–109
  targeted firms and counties, 89–90, 91

Business incentives, national interests in actual *vs.* ideal incentive practice and, 107–108
  enlarging the national economy with, 104–106
  help for distressed regions and, 111–114, 114*b*, 136–137*n*141, 137*nn*142–144
  solving regressive income distribution with, 108–109, 136*nn*132–135
  state sovereignty balanced with, 102, 109–111, 136*nn*136–140
  U.S. potential role in state and local incentives, 101–102
  zero-sum game of state and local competition, 102–104, 135*nn*128–130
Business incentives, practical reform of, 115–120
  alternatives to present tax incentives, 118–119, 137*nn*149–150
  better evaluation to accompany transparency, 116–117, 118, 137*nn*147–148
  danger in, *vs.* keeping what is still worth keeping, 120
  full employment economy and, 119, 120, 137*nn*151–152
  transparency, 115–116, 137*nn*145–146
Business incentives evaluation, 61–88
  applying national studies to, 81–86, 84*b*, 85*b*, 87, 87*b*, 133–134*n*114, 133*nn*111–113, 134*nn*115-116
  benefits and costs in, 17, 117, 123*n*22
  different models for, 36–37, 61–63, 125*n*37, 126–127*n*56, 126*n*55, 127*n*57, 131*nn*92–93
  factors affecting benefits in, 26–34, 124*nn*29–35, 125*nn*36–46, 126*nn*47–52
  factors affecting costs in, 34–35, 126*nn*53–54
  leakages and negative feedbacks (costs) in, 22–26, 23*f*, 123–124*n*28, 123*n*27

Business incentives evaluation, *cont.*
  methodology decisions in, 69, 69*b*,
    74–77, 75*b*–76*b*, 86–88, 87*b*
  multipliers and spillovers (benefits)
    in, 18–22, 19*f*, 27–29, 123*nn*23–
    26, 125*nn*36–43
  scoring in, 70–73, 74, 77, 113,
    132*n*105, 224*b*
  selection bias challenge in, 63–64
  selection bias minimized in, 64–77
    (*see also under* Research
    implementation)
  surveys in, 77–81, 80*b*, 81*b*,
    132*nn*106–107, 133*nn*108–110
Business taxes
  actual, and incentives package limits,
    93, 135*n*121
  extra, proposed on incentives, 109,
    136*n*133
  financing incentives with, 55*t*, 58,
    81–82, 83, 133*n*111, 134*n*116
  job creation and, incentives, 90, 95

California
  film tax credits in, and RCT
    evaluation, 132*n*96
  high-tech area in, 5, 28, 112, 125*n*40,
    137*n*142
Cash grants, 1, 80*b*
  block, as federal programs, 112–113,
    114*b*
  as job creation incentive, 8, 9*f*, 78,
    83, 85*b*
  targeted counties with, 91–92, 112
Clinton administration, Empowerment
  Zone program under, 77,
  132*n*105
Colorado, high-tech area in, 28, 125*n*40
Community colleges
  job training at, as business incentive,
    1, 9–10, 31
  workforce programs at, 50, 55*t*
Community development, neighborhoods
  and, 2, 77, 121*nn*2–4, 132*n*105
Commuting zone (CZ), employment
  rates and job relocation in, 113,
  137*n*143

Competition, 4
  interstate political, and business
    incentives, 3, 5, 7, 28, 99, 101–
    102, 125*n*37
  local, on attracting businesses, 5, 12,
    24, 35
  zero-sum game of state and local
    incentives, and U.S. interests,
    102–104, 135*nn*128–130
Connecticut, move away from incentives
  evaluation with "but for"
  percentage by, 36–37, 126–
  127*n*56
Corporate businesses, 11, 90
  added value of, and discount
    calculations, 83, 84*b*, 133*n*113
  incentive access knowledge by, 13, 96
  income tax liabilities of, and state
    incentives, 8–9
  large, and national interests, 104,
    110–111, 113–114, 114*b*, 115,
    135*n*130, 136*nn*138–140
  multipliers for, *vs.* local businesses,
    28–29
  out-of-state, and benefit receipt, 18,
    26, 124*n*31
  short-term focus *vs.* long-term
    incentives for, 24, 26, 113–114,
    120, 124*nn*32–34
  state income tax revenue from, and
    incentive costs, 10, 122*n*11
Customized business services
  as alternative to present tax
    incentives, 118, 119
  cash grants for, 91–92
  higher, benefit-cost ratios with,
    94–95
  local businesses and, 90, 119
  national economy and, 101, 104–105,
    112
  taxes on, 109, 136*n*133
Customized job training, 118
  distressed areas and, 112, 136–
    137*n*141
  as incentives, 27, 31, 124*n*35
  program evaluation of, 66, 79, 80*b*,
    132*n*98, 132*n*107, 133*n*108

CZ. *See* Commuting zone

Dallas area, high-tech industries in, 125*n*40
Demand-side financing, effects on consumers of, 34–35
Denver area, high-tech industries in, 28, 125*n*40
Distressed areas
   business incentives for, (jobless) compared by state, 13–14, 123*n*19
   Empowerment and Opportunity Zone programs for, 77, 132*n*105
   European Union caps on incentives in, 109, 136*nn*134–135
   federal costs for job help to, 113, 114*b*, 137*nn*143–144
   help for, and national interest, 111–114, 120, 136–137*n*141, 137*nn*142–144
   Michigan counties as, and hypothetical program effects using RDD, 75*b*–76*b*, 76*f*
   social benefits in, and business incentives, 13–14, 29, 70–71, 95, 125*n*43
   targeted incentives in, with higher returns, 96, 98, 105–106

Economic benefits with incentives, 36, 94
   maximized, for state residents, 89, 98
Economic development, basic services that support, 91, 104–106
Economic development incentives
   aim of, 1, 2–3, 19*f*
   definition of, 1–2, 121*n*2
   escalation of, 1, 7–8, 8*f*, 121*n*1
   evaluation of, 6, 15, 17, 61
   targeted, and reasons for, 3–5, 120
   as wasteful, 5–6, 115
   See also entries beginning Business incentives
Economic development plans
   assumptions in some, 37, 127*n*57
   Brookings Institution program as, 30, 126*n*47
   buzzwords in, 45, 129*nn*75–78
   as distinguished from neighborhood plans, 2, 121*nn*2–4
   funding mix for services in, 9*f*, 10
   geographic areas selected for, 67, 73, 77, 132*n*105
   Minnesota programs as, 32, 126*n*50, 134*n*118
   U.S. programs as, 110–111, 131*n*96
Education programs
   high-quality, *vs.* average incentives, 53–54
   K–12 public schools, 50*f*, 51–53, 130*n*84
   preschool, of high quality, 49–50, 50*f*, 94, 132*n*102
   RDD application to incentive evaluation of, 71, 132*nn*102–103
   scholarship awards, 50*f*, 51
   Talent 2025 and local skill development as, 119
   See also Community colleges; Michigan State University; Virginia Polytechnic Institute and State University
Employment, local, and in-migrant workers, 5, 25, 29–30, 62, 125*n*45
Employment rates
   commuting zone, and job relocation, 113, 137*n*143
   earnings and, 43, 46, 128*n*70
   as employment-to-population ratio, 14, 75*b*–76*b*, 96, 123*n*20
   job creation and, 6, 20, 29–32, 125*nn*44–46, 126*nn*47–50
Empowerment Zone program, for distressed geographic areas, 77, 132*n*105
Enterprise zones, in local jobless markets, 14, 123*n*21
   See also Opportunity Zones
Entrepreneurship training, 10, 131*n*96
Environmental concerns, job growth and potential for, 17
European Union
   caps (limits) on cost per job created, 92, 134*n*119

Index 155

European Union, *cont.*
  incentive regulatory system in, 109, 136*nn*134–135

Federal programs
  block grants as, 112–113, 114*b*
  funding mix with, for economic development services, 9*f*, 10
  infrastructure investments by, 48–49, 129*n*81
  (*see also specifics, e.g.,* Tennessee Valley Authority [TVA])
  job help costs to, in distressed areas, 113, 137*nn*143–144
  local market benefits of, *vs.* neighborhoods, 2, 121*n*4
  potential role of, in state and local incentives (*see* Business incentives, national interests in)
Financing incentives
  better, policies with fewer in-state burdens, 57–58
  with business taxes, 55*t*, 58, 90–91
  demand- *vs.* supply-side, 34–35
  household taxes for, 40, 103, 127*n*63, 129–130*n*83, 136*n*131
  opportunity costs of, incentives, 51–53, 117, 130*n*84
  with public spending cuts, 51–53, 55*t*, 90, 120
  voter awareness of, 115–116
  welfare and social programs cuts for, 44, 128*n*74
Foxconn (firm)
  business incentives offered to, 1, 9, 12, 13, 27, 97, 122*n*9, 135*n*124
  evaluation of, deal with "but for" percentage, 36–37, 126–127*n*56, 134*n*115
  evaluation of incentives deal with, 36, 126*n*55
  U.S. location potential for, 102, 135*n*128
Free services, attracting businesses with, 1
Funders' Network, "inclusive growth" as buzzword to, 45, 129*n*77

GASB. *See* Government Accounting Standards Board
GDP. *See* Gross Domestic Product
Geographic areas
  counties and metropolitan areas as, 32–33, 44, 91, 95–96, 126*n*51, 128*n*73
  economic development plans selected for, 67, 73, 77, 108–109, 113, 132*n*105
  (*see also* Distressed areas)
Google (firm), poaching workers by, 20, 123*n*25
Government Accounting Standards Board (GASB), mandate for incentive dollar cost disclosure by, 116, 137*n*146
Government subsidies to firms. *See* Subsidies
Grand Rapids, Michigan, economic development strategies for, 118–119, 137*n*149
Gross Domestic Product (GDP), damage to U.S., 112

High-tech industries
  communities with, and above average population, 28, 90, 125*nn*39–41
  firms in tradable, targeted for business incentives, 89–90, 106
  multiplier effect of, 5, 20, 28, 55*t*, 91, 123*nn*25–26, 125*nn*39–41, 131*n*94
  R&D tax credits for, 9, 68*b*, 117
  strengthening cluster development of, 112, 113, 136–137*n*141, 137*n*142
Hiring subsidies
  as employer incentive, 31–32, 56–57, 126*nn*49–50, 130*n*89
  in ideal incentive program, 92, 134*n*118
Household taxes
  assumption of financing incentives with, 40, 103, 136*n*131
  benefit-cost ratio and, incentive financing, 127*n*63, 129–130*n*83
Housing supply, shortage of, 112

Illinois, 113
employment rate and incentives in, vs. Indiana, 14, 123n20
evaluation of manufacturing extension services in, 79, 132n106
Income
incentive benefits distributed across, groups, 43–45, 43f, 106–107, 120, 128nn70–74, 129nn75–78, 136n131
per capita, affected by state incentives, 8–9, 17, 21–22, 25, 42, 42t, 50, 50f, 94, 117
solving regressive, distribution with national interests, 108–109, 135n129, 136nn132–135
Income taxes, corporate business liabilities for, 8–9
Indiana, employment rate and incentives in, vs. Illinois, 14, 123n20
Infrastructure
adequate, as basic service supporting economic development, 91, 93–94
development programs for, as alternative to present tax incentives, 118, 119
federal investment in, 48–49, 129n81
funding for, in distressed areas, 112, 136–137n141
spending for, 22, 25, 33–34, 35, 36
Investment, 35, 120
effect of, by large corporations, 110, 136n137
federal, in infrastructure, 48–49, 129n81
future discounted in business, decisions, 82–83
social discount rates and, decisions, 54, 130n85
tax credits for, as state business incentives, 9, 9f

Job creation, 17, 44
cost per job created, 79, 85–86, 90, 92, 120, 132nn106–107, 133n108, 134nn119–120

credits for, as largest business incentive, 8–9, 9f, 84b
effect of, on state economies, 61–63, 117
employment rates and, 6, 29–32, 125nn44–46, 126nn47–50
infrastructure programs for, 48–49, 129n81
local, required of state incentives, 18–21, 19f
new jobs for state residents vs. in-migrants and policy, 30–32, 62, 126nn47–50
selection bias challenge and, in business incentives evaluation, 63–64
share of new jobs in-state with better incentive policies, 56–57, 89, 130–131nn90–91, 130n89
targeted incentives for, and economic rationale, 4–5
Job growth, 17
claimed vs. actual, 79, 107–108, 133n109
effects of incentives associated with (see Business incentives evaluation)
hypothetical, program and RDD effects, 75b–76b, 76f
inclusivity of, 45, 129nn74–78
local brownfield redevelopment and, 48, 129n81
promotion of, 2–3, 7, 20–21, 36, 113, 120, 121n2, 135n129
Job opportunities, full-employment economy and, 119
Job skills, added, as incentives benefit, 20
Job training
benefit-cost ratios of, 55t, 57, 130–131n90, 131n91
cuts in, and future wages, 25–26
free, as business incentive, 1, 9–10
nonemployed workers and, 105–106, 113
See also Customized job training
Jobs, 1, 3
federal costs for, in needy areas, 113, 137nn143–144

Index 157

Jobs, *cont.*
  numbers of, and incentives, 26, 115, 117, 124*n*30
  public and private, in distressed areas, 112, 136–137*n*141

Labor markets
  excess supply in, and economically depressed areas, 30–31, 126*n*48
  local, and in-migrant workers, 5, 25, 62
  local *vs.* neighborhood, 2, 121*nn*2–4
  policy for, to include business incentives, 42, 45, 117, 120
Land, attracting businesses with, 1, 7, 118, 122*n*8
  See also entries beginning, Property
Loans, attracting businesses with, 1, 131*n*95
Local businesses
  competition among, 5, 12
  customized services for, 90, 119
  federal programs and, *vs.* neighborhoods, 2, 121*n*4
  incentives receipt by, 18, 55*t*, 123*n*24, 124*n*31
  multipliers average higher for, 28–29, 125*n*42
  small, assistance in distressed areas, 112, 115, 136–137*n*141
Local economies
  economic development strategies for, 118–119
  infrastructure for, 33–34, 35, 48, 119
  job numbers in, 42, 45
  size of, 32–33, 126*n*51
Local governments, 3
  advisory services of, 4, 27
  brownfield redevelopment by, 48, 129*n*81
  competition of, with state incentives, 101–104, 135*nn*128–130
  economic policies of, distinguished from business incentives, 2, 121*nn*2–4
  incentive deals disclosed by, 115–116, 137*nn*145–146
  officials in, affected by incentive politics, 3, 97, 115, 118, 119
  property tax abatement by, 9, 9*f*, 11
  sports teams subsidies by, 24, 123*n*17
  targeting and, 1, 12–13, 14, 91
  tax revenue *vs.* incentives cost and, 12, 95, 122*n*14

Manufacturing industries
  evaluation of extension services for, 66, 69, 79, 132*n*97, 132*n*101, 132*nn*106–107
  extension of, in distressed areas, 112, 115, 136–137*n*141
MBDP grants for job creation, 83, 85*b*, 88
Mississippi as leading state for, incentives, 7, 9, 122*n*8
  prioritized funding for extension services to, 91–92, 118–119
Maryland, move away from incentives evaluation with "but for" percentage by, 36–37, 126–127*n*56
Massachusetts, evaluation of customized job training in, 79, 80*b*, 88, 132*n*107
MBDP. *See* Michigan Business Development Program
Media attention
  business incentives and, 13, 90, 97
  Wikipedia as, 45, 129*n*78
MEED. *See* Minnesota Employment and Economic Development program
Metropolitan areas
  job growth in, and income quintiles, 44, 128*n*73
  too big to be "local economy," 32–33, 126*n*51
Metropolitan Policy Program, achieving more inclusive economic development with, 30, 126*n*47
Michigan, 7
  assistance to distressed counties in, and hypothetical program effects using RDD, 75*b*–76*b*, 76*f*, 113

Michigan, *cont.*
    investments by, in manufacturing areas, 118–119
    job creation grant program (MBDP) in, 83, 85*b*, 88
Michigan State University, medical school of, and local business, 119
Minge, Rep. David, extra business taxes on incentives proposal by, 109, 136*n*133
Minneapolis-St. Paul area, high-tech industries in, 28, 125*n*40
Minnesota
    economic development plans (MEED) in, 32, 126*n*50, 134*n*118
    high-tech area in, 28, 125*n*40
Mississippi, as leading state with business incentives, 7, 9, 122*n*8
Multiplier effects, 6, 125*n*37
    assumption of, in basic incentives model, 40, 127*n*62
    benefit-cost ratio and, 56, 127*n*63, 130*n*88
    high-tech clusters and, 89–90
    job creation and, 4–5, 20, 46, 58, 62, 121*n*6, 131*n*94
    overstatement of, 5, 27–28, 117, 125*n*36
    spillovers and, (benefits) in evaluation, 18–22, 19*f*, 27–29, 123*nn*23–26, 125*nn*36–43

Neighborhoods
    community development of, 2, 121*nn*2–4
    not large enough per se to be "local economy," 32–33, 126*n*52
New Mexico, business incentives in, *vs.* national average, 13
New York (state)
    Amazon business location decision with, 97–98, 116, 135*n*125
    evaluation of Amazon deal with "but for" percentage by, 36–37, 126–127*n*56
    incentives offered in, 7, 8*f*
Nontradable goods or services
    local firms in, 12, 24, 35

multipliers and, *vs.* tradable, 4–5, 24, 123–124*n*28
North Carolina
    employment rate and incentives in, *vs.* South Carolina, 14, 123*n*20
    geographic areas tiered for incentives eligibility in, 70, 98, 135*n*127

Opportunity costs
    financing, with school spending cuts, 51–53
    incentives with, 34–35, 117
Opportunity Zone program
    for distressed geographic areas, 77, 132*n*105
    local market benefits of, *vs.* neighborhoods, 2, 121*n*4
    See also Enterprise zones

Pew Charitable Trusts
    state evaluation examples provided by, 61, 131*nn*92–93
    tax credit demise recommendation by, 117, 137*n*148
    tax incentive budget caps and, 95, 135*n*123
Politics and business incentives, 3, 121*n*5
    ideal relationship of, 89, 97–98
    interstate competition in, 3, 5, 7
    likelihood of federal impositions on states, 109–11, 136*nn*136–140
    offsetting influences in, 7, 115, 119
    paying for long-term costs, 14–15
    surveys in evaluations and, 77–78
    voter awareness of, 13, 90, 97, 115–116, 118, 137*nn*145–146
Population growth
    areas with, 28, 90, 125*n*40
    public services needs and, 43, 62, 128*n*67
Private employers, 3
    favored for business incentives, 13, 123*n*18
    job growth promotion by, 2–3, 121*n*2, 135*n*129
Productivity, U.S., 112, 113
Property taxes, abatement of hypothetical value-added per worker and, 86*b*, 134*n*115

Index 159

Property taxes, *cont.*
  local government and, 9, 9*f*, 11, 34, 94*t*
Property values, incented job growth and, 21, 42, 42*t*, 128*n68*
Public policy
  clawbacks in, 26–27, 54–55, 93, 96–97, 124*n*32, 135*n*122
  effect of state incentives evaluation on, 131*n*92
  effects of, on business incentives, 25–35, 55*t*, 59
  federal, as carrots *vs.* sticks, 110–111, 113–114
  ideal, about incentives, 6, 39, 88 (*see also* Business incentives, ideal state program)
  long-term *vs.* up-front business incentives and, 14–15, 47, 54–55, 55*t*, 90, 129*n80*
  new jobs for state residents *vs.* in-migrants, 30–32, 62, 126*nn*47–50
Public services
  cost of wasteful incentives to, 5–6, 117
  education programs as, 49–51, 50*f*, 130*n*84
  needs for, and population, 43, 62, 128*n*67
  spending for, 5–6, 22, 25–26, 34, 35, 36, 62, 90
  targeted business incentives and, 1, 12, 122*n*16
  tax revenue *vs.* incentives cost and, 12, 122*n*14, 122*n*16

Quality of life, incentives affect on, 17, 25

Randomized controlled trials (RCT)
  accidental, via lottery, 132*n*96
  research implementation to minimize bias, 65, 86, 87*b*, 131–132*n*96, 131*n*95
RCT. *See* Randomized controlled trials
R&D. *See* Research and Development within firms

RDD. *See* Regression-discontinuity design
Regional Economics Model Incorporated (REMI), cluster and cost feedback effects in, 125*n*37, 131*n*94
Regression-discontinuity design (RDD)
  application of, to incentive evaluation and preschools, 71, 132*nn*102–103
  estimating a program's effect at cutoff, 71, 76*f*, 113, 114*b*
  as type of quasi-experiment, 70–71, 73–77, 75*b*–76*b*, 77*b*, 86, 87*b*, 132*nn*104–105
REMI. *See* Regional Economics Model Incorporated
Research and Development (R&D) within firms
  investment in, and market power of large corporations, 110, 136*n*137
  spending in chemicals and computer manufacturing industries for, 13, 122–123*n*17
  tax credits for, as state business incentives, 9, 9*f*, 67, 68*b*, 132*n*99
  tax credits for, spending as state business incentives, 9, 9*f*, 117
Research implementation, 64–77
  designed quasi-experiments, 70–77, 75*b*–76*b*, 77*b*, 132*nn*102–105
  natural experiments, 65–69, 68*b*, 69*b*, 86, 87*b*, 132*nn*95–101
  quasi-experiments, 65–77
  RCT to minimize bias, 65, 131–132*n*96, 131*n*95
  sample size in, 67, 73–74
  selection bias and other problems in, 63–64, 74, 83
Rhode Island, move away from incentives evaluation with "but for" percentage by, 36–37, 126–127*n*56

Silicon Valley, 5
  above average population in, 28, 125*n*40
  growth restrictions due to housing supply shortage in, 112, 137*n*142

Skills development programs
  as alternative to present tax incentives, 118, 119, 120
  as basic service supporting economic development, 91, 93–94, 112
  better policies than average business incentives lie in, 49–51, 50*f,* 129–130*n*83, 129*n*82
  high-quality, *vs.* average incentives, 53–54
  See also Education programs; Job training
Social benefits, 3
  business incentives and, to needy areas, 13–14, 29, 70–71, 125*n*43
  costs of, 5–6, 26, 124*n*33
  as economic rationale for business incentives, 4–5, 121*n*2
Social programs
  benefits distribution of expanded economy to, 106, 136*n*131
  financing incentives with cuts to, 44, 128*n*74
  see also Welfare programs
South Carolina, employment rate and incentives in, *vs.* North Carolina, 14, 123*n*20
Sports teams, government subsidies for, 24, 74, 77, 123*n*17
State economies, 59
  effect of incented firms' job growth on, 61–63
  effects of paying for incentive costs on, 34–35, 117, 126*nn*53–55
State governments, 112
  advisory services of, 4, 10, 27, 55–56, 72
  budgeting by, 90, 94*t,* 95, 135*n*123
  customized services of, 27, 79, 88, 90, 94*t,* 95
  economic policies of, distinguished from business incentives, 2, 121*n*2
  federal takeover of, 108–111, 136*nn*132–140
  incentive deals disclosed by, 115–116, 137*nn*145–146
  incentives designed by, 6, 9, 15, 63–64, 83, 89, 90, 134*n*116
  (*see also* Business incentives, ideal state programs; Mississippi; Washington (state); *and specific names of states, e.g.,* Illinois)
  officials in, affected by incentive politics, 3, 14, 90, 96–97, 113, 115, 118, 119
  targeted business incentives by, 1, 9–10, 12–13, 96
  tax revenue *vs.* incentives cost and, 3, 12, 17, 122*n*14
State legislative oversight, 36–37, 126–127*n*56
  interstate compacts as, 119, 137*nn*151–152
  Washington State Legislative Audit and Review Commission, 117
  Wisconsin Legislative Fiscal Bureau, 36, 126*n*55
Subsidies, 103
  discretionary hiring and, 31–32, 56–57, 92, 126*nn*49–50, 130*n*89, 134*n*118
  equal, for capital and labor as ideal incentive, 92–93, 134*n*120
  private, for jobs in distressed areas, 112, 136–137*n*141
  for sports teams, 24, 74, 77, 123*n*17
  to state businesses and interstate commerce, 109, 136*n*132
  as wages to firms, 11, 12, 27, 122*n*12, 122*nn*15–16
Supply-side financing, effects on state economy of, 34–35
Surveys
  in business incentives evaluation, 77–81, 87, 87*b*
  factors enhancing credibility of, 80–81, 81*b,* 132*nn*106–107, 133*n*110
  reported cost per job created, 79, 132*nn*106–107, 133*n*108

Tax breaks
  attracting businesses with, 1, 39–40
  cutback of, 7, 115, 119, 120, 137*n*151

Tax breaks, *cont.*
  discretionary *vs.* universal, 94*t*, 112–113, 114*b*, 121*n*2
  as job creation credit, 8, 9*f*, 78
Tax credits
  as entitlements, 94*t*, 113
  evaluation of, for California films by RCT, 132*n*96
  hypothetical value-added per worker and, 86*b*, 134*n*115
  investment and R&D, as state business incentives, 9, 9*f*, 67, 68*b*, 92, 117, 132*n*99
  job creation, for tradable industries, 92–93, 134*n*120
Tax revenue, 62
  fiscal gain of incentives and, 5–6, 21–22, 33–34, 66
  incentives cost and, 12, 25, 122*n*14
  increases in, 3, 34
Taxes. *See specifics, e.g.,* Business taxes; Household taxes; Income taxes; Property taxes
Tennessee Valley Authority (TVA)
  evaluation of, as economic development program, 67, 131*n*100
  federal costs for, 113, 137*n*144
  as federal infrastructure investment, 48, 129*n*81
Texas, high-tech area in, 28, 125*n*40
Tradable goods or services
  firms with, targeted for business incentives, 8*f*, 12–13, 35, 89–90, 102–103, 122–123*n*17
  industries with, and job creation tax credits, 92–93, 134*n*120
  nontradable *vs.,* and multipliers, 4–5, 24, 123–124*n*28
Transportation programs, as federal infrastructure investment in local development, 48, 94
Trump administration, help for distressed regions under, 77, 111–114, 132*n*105
TVA (Tennessee Valley Authority), 48, 67, 129*n*81, 131*n*100
Twin Cities area. *See* Minneapolis-St. Paul area

Unemployment, worker history of, and hiring potential, 31–32, 91–92, 126*nn*49–50, 134*n*118
Unemployment rate
  assumption of, in basic incentives model, 40, 127*n*61
  benefit-cost ratio and, 56–57, 127*n*63, 130*n*89
  low, and business incentives, 95, 119
United States (U.S.)
  business incentives (*see under* Business incentives, national interests in; Federal programs)
  federal regulations in, 101–102, 109, 110, 136*n*132
  government accounting mandates in, 116, 137*n*146
  interstate compacts in, 119, 137*n*151
  productivity of, 112, 113
U.S. Congress, business tax proposals in, 109, 136*n*133
U.S. Supreme Court, business incentive challenges in, 109, 136*n*136

Virginia
  Amazon business location decision with, 97–98, 116, 135*nn*125–126
  evaluation of Amazon deal with "but for" percentage by, 36–37, 126–127*n*56
Virginia Polytechnic Institute and State University, Amazon location deal and, 98, 135*n*126

Wages
  boost in, and job growth, 20–21, 120
  incentive for, *vs.* profit gaps, 11–12
  job training and, 25–26, 80*b*
  real, as share of increased earnings, 43, 46, 128*n*70
  reduced upward, 5, 7, 25, 110
  state subsidies to firms for, 11, 12, 27, 122*n*12, 122*nn*15–16
Washington (state), 13
  R&D tax credit evaluation for high-tech industries in, 68*b*, 117, 137*n*147

Welfare programs
  benefits distribution of expanded economy to, 106, 136*n*131
  financing incentives with cuts to, 44, 128*n*74
West Michigan Medical Device Consortium, local business development behind, 119, 137*n*150
Wisconsin, 7
  business incentives provided by, 1, 12, 13, 27.97
  evaluation of Foxconn deal with "but for" percentage by, 36–37, 126–127*n*56, 126*n*55, 134*n*115
Workforce Training Fund Program, evaluation in and by Massachusetts of, 79, 80*b*, 88, 132*n*107
World Bank, "inclusive growth" as buzzword to, 45, 129*n*75

"Your State's Name Here" (Berryman and Berryman), 11–12, 122*n*13

Zero-sum game
  state and local incentive competition of national interest, 102–104, 135*nn*128–130

About the Institute

The W.E. Upjohn Institute for Employment Research is a nonprofit research organization devoted to finding and promoting solutions to employment-related problems at the national, state, and local levels. It is an activity of the W.E. Upjohn Unemployment Trustee Corporation, which was established in 1932 to administer a fund set aside by Dr. W.E. Upjohn, founder of The Upjohn Company, to seek ways to counteract the loss of employment income during economic downturns.

The Institute is funded largely by income from the W.E. Upjohn Unemployment Trust, supplemented by outside grants, contracts, and sales of publications. Activities of the Institute comprise the following elements: 1) a research program conducted by a resident staff of professional social scientists; 2) the Early Career Research Award program, which provides funding for emerging scholars to complete policy-relevant research on labor-market issues; 3) a publications program and online research repository, which provide a vehicles for disseminating the research of staff and outside scholars; 4) a regional team that conducts analyses for local economic and workforce development; and 5) the Employment Management Services Division, which administers publicly funded employment and training services as Michigan Works! Southwest in the Institute's local four-county area.

The broad objectives of the Institute's activities are to 1) promote scholarship and evidence-based practices on issues of employment and unemployment policy, and 2) make knowledge and scholarship relevant and useful to policymakers in their pursuit of solutions related to employment and unemployment.

Current areas of concentration for these programs include the causes, consequences, and measures to alleviate unemployment; social insurance and income maintenance programs; compensation and benefits; workforce skills; nonstandard work arrangements; and place-based policy initiatives for strengthening regional economic development and local labor markets.

CPSIA information can be obtained
at www.ICGtesting.com
Printed in the USA
FFHW010814121019
55526851-61329FF

9 780880 996686